Crushing the
Spirits *of* Greed
and Poverty

Crushing the Spirits *of* Greed *and* Poverty

Discerning and Defeating the Ancient Powers
of Mammon and Babylon

SANDIE FREED

Chosen
a division of Baker Publishing Group
Grand Rapids, Michigan

Published by Chosen Books
a division of Baker Publishing Group
P.O. Box 6287, Grand Rapids, MI 49516-6287
www.chosenbooks.com

Printed in the United States of America

Library of Congress Cataloging-in-Publication Data
Freed, Sandie, 1951–
    Crushing the spirits of greed and poverty : discerning and defeating the ancient powers of mammon and Babylon / Sandie Freed.
        p.   cm.
    Includes bibliographical references.
    ISBN 978-0-8007-9490-3 (pbk.)
    1. Avarice—Religious aspects—Christianity. 2. Poverty—Religious aspects—Christianity. I. Title.
    BV4627.A8F74 2010
    241'.68—dc22   2010008904

10   11   12   13   14   15   16   7   6   5   4   3   2   1

Contents

Foreword by Chuck D. Pierce   7
Acknowledgments   13
Introduction   15

1. God and Mammon   21
2. Babylon and Wealth   43
3. Iniquity, Tyre and Seats of Authority   65
4. Understanding the Deceitfulness of Riches   91
5. Our Treasure Is Where Our Hearts Are   109
6. Is There an Ammonite in Your Treasury?   133
7. Anointed to Defeat Mammon, Babylon and Divination   149
8. It Is Written!   171
9. Too Close to Home   191
10. Repairing the Altar of God   205

Notes   215

5

Foreword

I n this "season of seeing," our materialistic society must look at and contend with the greatest spirit holding us in captivity: *poverty*. We are at war to see poverty break. If you are sent to war but lose the battle, you wear reproach until you gain a subsequent victory. Many in the Body of Christ are afraid to war—but war is necessary in order to conquer our enemies and take possession of what has been promised us. War is receiving grace to fight (see 1 Timothy 6:12; 2 Timothy 2:3–4). War is receiving the necessary armor for victory (see Ephesians 6:11–16). And war produces an opportunity for us to enter into victory (see Revelation 3:21).

This wonderful book by Sandie Freed is a war manual. *Crushing the Spirits of Greed and Poverty* defines an enemy and gives a strategy for contending.

Poverty is refusing to become what God has created and destined us to be. It includes the mindset of not believing that the Lord can branch us into the fullness of His plan.

Poverty is not just experiencing lack, but *fearing* that we will lack. It occurs when we conform our circumstances to the blueprint given us by the world and we never see who God really made us to be. Poverty occurs when the god of this world surrounds and influences us with the world's perspective, causing us to forget God's ability in the midst of our circumstances. Poverty is the voice that says, "God is not able!"

Two of the most common means by which poverty takes hold are *oppression* and *wrong authoritative structures* (see Isaiah 5:8). Fear can cause us to develop a mentality of covetousness or gluttony that produces poverty (see Proverbs 23:21). Poverty causes us to become indolent or lazy (see Proverbs 24:33–34). Haste leads to poverty (see Proverbs 28:22), which occurs when we fall into get-rich-quick schemes. Poverty can also occur if we resist the Holy Spirit, thereby negating the blessings of the Lord.

What causes poverty in our lives? The main cause is failure to gather in the harvest, which sets a poverty mentality against us. Many times the enemy will wait until our harvest time to implement strategies of devastation against us. Like the Midianites who stole the harvest from the Israelites, the enemy has already devised a plan to eat up our assets and returns. We can plant. We can watch our crops grow. We can even enjoy a time of harvest. *But if we do not take our opportunity to gather and steward the harvest, a strategy of poverty will begin to develop against us.* When we increase without building storehouses to contain what we have harvested, the enemy will gain access to our excess and to our future.

We are required to combat poverty, then, by kindness and generosity to others. Like Boaz whose field Ruth visited, we combat poverty by allowing people to glean in our

8

vineyards and by providing them with access to our excess. We combat poverty by developing strategies to help those who have been ravaged by systemic poverty. In other words, we help others gain wisdom on how to break out of the system Satan is using to hold them captive financially. We are also required to develop reaping strategies (see Amos 9:13). When we do so, we overcome, and our increase goes from multiplication to multiplication.

This book will help you recognize a spirit of poverty that has held our generational bloodlines in captivity, keeping us from the fullness of the prosperity God has for us. The Lord is breaking in His people the power and practice of begging. He is making us people of faith. He will change the identity of His people from beggars to kings!

Crushing the Spirits of Greed and Poverty produces a decree in you that will cause you to command the power of poverty—and all the blindness that has invaded your atmosphere—to leave. Sandie leads us to take a passionate, even violent stand on behalf of the Body of Christ concerning this spirit. We must press through difficulties and storms to force an atmospheric change.

I declare that any atmosphere of poverty encircling you or your sphere of authority be invaded with the atmosphere of blessing and glory from heaven. Witness the glory of the Son of God, and then see how poverty is speaking to you. See past that spirit of poverty. Declare victory over the spirit of poverty. This evil spirit has violated God's perfect order and produced instability in many individuals. Restoration, biblically speaking, is always linked with multiplication. The Body of Christ needs to see restoration in our provision. Make a decree after reading this book that you will see all things restored.

Sandie's book is also about Mammon—a god that attempts to rule us by aligning with structures that cause interest rates to exceed godly bounds (see Nehemiah 5:1–5). Mammon creates fear and unwillingness to face our enemy (see Proverbs 22:13). Mammon causes us to succumb to persecution of faith (see 2 Corinthians 6 and 8). Mammon forces us into debt and financial defeat.

But God wants us to succeed. This book is filled with success and strategies for victory. Sandie uses key principles to help us overcome circumstances that would hold us captive and prevent us from bringing forth God's Kingdom plan. *To succeed* means to follow after, to dispossess the enemy and to possess or occupy his territory. It means to master the place or position the Lord assigns to us. Success occurs when we accomplish God's redemptive plan for our lives.

If we receive revelation, honor the prophets and are at the right place at the right time doing the right thing, we will succeed. Joshua 1:8 says:

> This Book of the Law shall not depart from your mouth, but you shall meditate in it day and night, that you may observe to do according to all that is written in it. For then you will make your way prosperous, and then you will have good success.
>
> Joshua 1:8, NKJV

Success occurs when we behave wisely, act prudently and study to develop skill and understanding. We already have help on our road to cause us to succeed!

In Deuteronomy 8 the Lord spoke to His covenant people, preparing them to go into the land He had promised them. He told them He was giving them the power to get wealth, but He also warned them about the pitfalls of worshiping Mammon—wealth with a debasing influence. God's assignment to Joshua and the tribes of Israel: to use their wealth for His Kingdom plan. To fulfill this assignment, a spiritual battle had to be fought, Mammon had to be defeated and all riches be transferred to God's rule and stewardship plan.

Proverbs 28:22 sheds some light by declaring that a man with an evil eye will greedily pursue earthly treasures. Matthew 6:24 explains that no one can serve both God and Mammon. Because we have a similar battle with Mammon today, Sandie's book is a must-read.

Money is in itself neither good nor bad. The key issue for us is our relationship and dedication to the power behind money. We must guard ourselves against the *love* of money (see 1 Timothy 6:10). The Greek word for "the love of money," *philarguria,* refers to avarice, which is covetousness, the insatiable greed for riches. It also means to inordinately or wrongly desire the possessions of others. If we are not careful, money will produce this fruit of covetousness in our hearts. The *deceitfulness of riches*—primarily a perceived power that comes with money—is another issue (see Mark 4:19). It produces an attitude of the heart that seeks to manipulate through false pretenses and appearances.

Sandie's book will produce in you a cry for an open heaven over your life, family, territory, business and ministry. Ask the Lord to shine His light on all darkness linked with the spirits being addressed here so you can see. When the windows of heaven open, every dark spiritual force that has trapped you in the past will flee. When the heavens open, the earth comes into divine realignment. When heavens open, men and women worship, and God renews covenant with them and with the earth. Mankind's authority activates God's power. He then wars on our behalf! Sandie's work will help produce a wind of change from an open heaven to blow upon us and produce victory. The defeat of the enemy occurs when we succeed in our struggle against some difficulty or obstacle impeding our path. Read *Crushing the Spirits of Greed and Poverty* and watch a victorious spirit rise within you!

Chuck D. Pierce
President, Global Spheres, Inc.
President, Glory of Zion International Ministries, Inc.
Watchman, Global Harvest Ministries

Acknowledgments

No journey I take into the revelatory realm would be successful without the love and support of my faithful intercessors. Daily they keep me covered in their prayers and empower me to peek into heaven and then write about what I see.

Thanks to my Zion Family who, through their faithfulness and commitment, keep the ministry going in the Bedford, Texas, area. Truly you all are the ones who make our First Friday Fire happen.

I wish to thank my spiritual parents, Bishop and "Mom" Evelyn, for their guidance and impartation into my life for more than 25 years. And, thank you, Papa, for your endorsement of this book and always being there for me.

I honor my faithful friends Dr. Jim and Jeanni Davis for their wisdom and encouragement. And a special thank you to Dr. Jim for his theological insight throughout this book.

Acknowledgments

I wish once again to thank my friend and co-laborer Apostle Chuck Pierce for committing to write another foreword. Chuck's incredible, cutting-edge ministry has empowered me to climb to greater heights in revelation.

I want to thank my special friends Jane Campbell, editorial director, and editor Grace Sarber for working with me on another project. Here we go, girls—one more time!

And always, I honor my husband, Mickey, for believing there is still more in me to give out to others. Mickey, thank you for never allowing me to settle for less than God's best for me.

Introduction

A deep-throated, gurgling, hissing sound defiled the atmosphere. The horrifying noise seemed to be coming from beneath my bed. Suddenly a firm grip by a large hand grabbed my right foot and began to pull me down and out of bed. The hideous sound grew louder as this evil force pulled me down and closer to its face. I was trembling with fear, fighting for my life. I tried to scream for help from my husband, Mickey. I tried to cry out for rescue, but the words remained captive inside my mind. The gurgling and hissing grew still louder. I barely glanced below to get a glimpse of what lay beneath. A dark hole with flames! *My Lord! The devil is trying to pull me down into hell!* I dared not look down to see the face of the evil thing! *God, please don't let me see his demonic face. I know it is much too evil even to imagine!* Finally the scream came. "Mickey, help me!"

Mickey jolted from the bed praying. I shared the horror I had experienced.

It seemed so real. Thank God it was a dream. The room was darker than the normal darkness of night, for a spirit of darkness overshadowed me.

Never seeing the face of my enemy, I knew why it was there. For weeks I had been receiving heavenly downloads concerning the spirit of Mammon. Being a prophet and revelatory in gifting, I love to pen what the Lord reveals. I am confident that part of my godly purpose in life is to be a voice for Him, whether through writing, preaching, teaching or simply sharing the Gospel. At first I was excited to be allowed to "see" some of the mysteries God has given me to share with you. I have to confess, however, that though I have written many books and articles that expose the plans of Satan, this project has been the most difficult to author.

As you continue to read you will understand why the enemy does not desire for this particular book to be written. You will discover with each chapter that Mammon affects everything in our lives.

Mammon is not simply a love of money; rather, it is a demonic spirit that attempts to set itself up as equal to God. Jesus said, "You cannot serve God and Mammon" (see Matthew 6:24; Luke 16:13). He is quite clear in His statement: God is God, and the opposite of God is Mammon. A clear choice is involved. To be blunt, I believe that if we are not serving God, then most likely we are serving Mammon. This book will help you understand how Mammon enslaves and imprisons us if we trust in worldly riches. The bottom line is: It is about who or what we trust.

On a scale of 1 to 10 (10 being most evil), the spirit of Mammon is a 9.999! Our entire world operates around money. Is it any wonder that an idol was created that men would worship above the One True God? Satan planned this evil scheme ever since he crawled on his belly as a snake in the Garden of Eden. Since we must have finances to survive, Satan capitalized on this evil and seduced mankind to worship money. And whenever we put our trust in money rather than God, we fall prey to the enemy over and over again.

Let me warn you ahead of time that this book may challenge your present theology concerning wealth and riches—especially when I refer to Mammon as a named evil spirit behind the idolatry of money. Mammon is the name of an ancient idol, and since demonic spirits are behind every idol and form of idol worship, we can conclude that Mammon can also be an evil spirit. I therefore use a capital *M* when I am discussing the false god actually named "Mammon" and the spirit behind it, as well as worldly riches or ungodly wealth. I also will use the phrase "the spirit of Mammon," which refers to the demonic forces behind the false god of Mammon that still influence us today.

Please do not allow your past understanding of Mammon to sabotage fresh revelation concerning the spirit behind deceitful riches. Can we agree together that God is unfolding hidden mysteries, especially now that we are in the end times? It is important to recognize the spiritual climate of the day and be as the Issachar tribe, which discerned God's times and seasons. Precious ones, this is our season to be freed from the bondage of Mammon.

Throughout this book I also will use the name Satan and devil interchangeably. They are one and the same. And let me say that I am not writing another book about the devil because I enjoy giving him attention. No way! My heart is to expose the enemy and see God's people set free. In reality, I much prefer to prophesy life. Yet many of us are blindsided daily by the adverse effects of Mammon. Not realizing the darkness connected to daily decisions regarding our finances opens the door to loss, hopelessness and death. The thief is stealing not only our destiny but also our blessings from us, and it is my intent to expose him and his cohorts, which include Mammon. The devil does not like exposure.

We are at war with evil. The enemy targets each one of us. As believers, we may as well get used to it. Satan's main goal is to steal worship from God by causing us to bow down to his plans. In doing so, we commit idolatry. One false god to whom we bow is Mammon. In bowing to him, we fall perfectly in line with Satan's plan to enslave us with bondage, take us completely out of God's perfect will and rob us of our inheritance and blessing.

It is a spiritual battle that manifests in the natural. To battle against this evil spirit, we must know our enemy and his tactics. Not to understand Satan's nature is merely to bat at the air and never give him a solid knockout punch. My goal is to equip you and to keep you from remaining ignorant of his evil devices. The only way to win the battle against Mammon is to be forewarned, forearmed and informed. By knowing and understanding his nature, we are winning the war.

As we proceed together on this journey, I want you to know that I have already talked to the Father about you. I have asked Him to reveal His heart concerning wealth and to open your eyes to see His goodness and love for you. I have prayed that you will completely put your trust in Him and not Mammon. I have also prayed Psalm 91 over your life, for the Lord to protect you and keep you from harm as the Holy Spirit directs your path and your future. I have also prayed for His seven-fold Spirit to be made manifest and to empower you to defeat your enemies. Mammon is our enemy, and I have asked the Lord to open our hearts, including mine, to reveal any hidden areas of darkness where He desires to bring forth light.

Precious ones, we cannot serve God and Mammon. Let us declare that we will serve only the One True God!

1

God and Mammon

You cannot serve God and mammon.

Matthew 6:24, NKJV

How magnificently this rich, young ruler was clothed! His garments, of the finest cloth, folded regally about him as he sat listening in amazement. *This Teacher is different*, thought the ruler. Jesus' words pierced the heart of the young man, who embraced every word and allowed each thought to penetrate deeply. He wanted the eternal life Jesus described. He earnestly desired the Kingdom of heaven.

Jesus' eyes rested a few moments on the young man, whose apparel and stateliness attracted everyone. His youth and eagerness to hear truth excited Jesus. Everywhere Jesus went He taught what was required to enter into the Kingdom of God. The young ruler wanted everything Jesus taught.

Little children were brought to Jesus. This intrigued the young ruler, who usually conversed only with those older, wiser and more prosperous. He had been taught that rulers rule over others and had little time for child's play.

But Jesus smiled and opened His arms to receive the children, and then He put His hand upon each of them to bless them. The little children were eager to touch Jesus and receive His attention. When the disciples rebuked the children, the young ruler agreed that they should not waste the Teacher's time. Jesus, on the other hand, said with compassion, " 'Let the little children come to Me, and do not forbid them; for of such is the kingdom of heaven.' And He laid His hands on them and departed from there" (Matthew 19:14–15, NKJV).

Is this also part of the Kingdom of heaven? the young ruler thought. *Talking to and embracing the children? I am so confused. His teachings are different from what I know. He does not seem like much of a ruler, but I can discern that He speaks with great authority. I am familiar with the Law, but it seems that I need something else to enter into this Kingdom of which the Teacher speaks. I will ask Him how to enter into this Kingdom.* He rose up and followed Jesus.

"Good Teacher, what good thing shall I do that I may have eternal life?"

Jesus replied, "If you want to enter into life, keep the commandments."

"Which ones?" the young man asked.

Jesus said, " 'You shall not murder,' 'You shall not commit adultery,' 'You shall not steal,' 'You shall not bear false witness,' 'Honor your father and your mother,' and 'You shall love your neighbor as yourself.' "

At first the young ruler was astounded. Jesus sounded nothing like the Pharisees who prayed endless prayers and made a spectacle of themselves. Their long, weary faces offered nothing desirable to this man. The young ruler eagerly replied, "All these things I have kept from my youth. What do I still lack?"

Jesus said to him, "If you want to be perfect, go, sell what you have and give to the poor, and you will have treasure in heaven; and come, follow Me."

When the young man heard that, his face fell, for he had great possessions. Jesus watched as the young ruler turned and left.

Jesus had not asked this requirement of every person He taught. So why did He require it of the young ruler? Jesus discerned that this extremely wealthy young man had bowed his knee to Mammon. Being a bond servant to riches had him completely imprisoned to a false god. And Jesus knew that a person cannot serve both God and Mammon.

Jesus said to His disciples:

> Assuredly, I say to you that it is hard for a rich man to enter the kingdom of heaven. And again I say to you, it is easier for a camel to go through the eye of a needle than for a rich man to enter the kingdom of God.
>
> Matthew 19:23–24, NKJV

The money test. Who can pass it? Have we allowed worry, anxiety and stress concerning money to turn us away from God? Do we trust more in riches than God? If so, then the false god Mammon is strapped tightly to us, and we must become disentangled from it in order to follow God and serve Him in His Kingdom.

Mixed Messages

Money and prosperity are hot topics today among believers. The message "No one can serve God and Mammon" has been coupled with another platform: "Money is the root of all evil." Both messages have been so misunderstood and misinterpreted that a number of Christians have settled into believing that they must choose either God or money and that they cannot have both in their lives. This is unscriptural.

The first message has led to a number of false beliefs, including, "I cannot have money and have a relationship with God," "If I serve God in any capacity, I cannot have money," and "If a person has great wealth, then God will not use him in ministry at all." None of these is true. Such false teachings and misunderstandings have led Christians to take pride in being poor, equating it somehow with holiness. Dear ones, suffering with poverty no more empowers us to be holy than having money defines us as being evil. In fact, poverty is part of a curse for rebellion and making foolish choices. These false beliefs lead not only to a poverty mentality, but also to a false belief system that God does not desire His people to be blessed. The devil would love for us to believe that we must be poor in order to be considered holy, but this is totally unscriptural! Look at Deuteronomy 28. God does want us blessed; He simply does not want money to become a false god in our lives.

Some extremists, on the other hand, declare by faith the "names and claims prosperity" and wait for money to fall

through the ceilings of their homes while remaining slothful and lazy and not working. This, too, is unscriptural. In
fact, Proverbs 12:24 states that the slothful man is placed
under tribute, meaning he is in bondage. Yes, the prosperity message has been taken to extremes—both positively
and negatively. The pendulum has swung both ways, and
so often our focus is wrong.

Your money is not evil. It is how you get it and how you
use it that can be defiling. It is the love of money that is the
root of evil. When we focus too much on money, prosperity
and wealth, we are listening to an evil spirit.

To a degree, we do have to make a choice, but not between God and money, as so many of us have been taught.
If money is an idol and we consider it our "source," then
yes, money is evil because we love it more than God. In
this case a choice between the two must be made.

Sounding the Alarm

Let me make it clear that I have no ulterior motive by writing this book on Mammon and Babylon. My heart is to
sound the alarm concerning idolatry and lead people to
true repentance if money has been their god. In writing this
book I am in no way advocating personal comfort, gain or
advancement. Rather, my heart is to make readers aware
that wealth is designed to build the Kingdom of God and
not our personal kingdoms.

Godly prosperity is not having wealth for the sake of
being wealthy, but rather having enough to fulfill our purposes in God. We are to use the prosperity God gives us
to promote His Kingdom and bless others along the way
so they can fulfill their purposes in God.

Our hearts can be deeply affected by money, both positively and negatively. You have heard it said before: "If you want to know where people's hearts are, just look at their checkbooks." I have begun to understand the deep truths held within this statement. I personally have come face-to-face with the spirit of Mammon, and let me tell you that I have never in my entire life struggled with trust in money or thoughts regarding finances as much as I have when I began writing this book. At first I wondered, *Could this struggle be due to our declining economy, or is it because I am close to entering retirement?* But I slowly began to realize that God had led me to this struggle in order to reach hearts.

I have learned that only through difficult times are we truly challenged to take a deep look into our hearts and motives and allow God to adjust us. He certainly has jerked me back into a deeper relationship with Him through the writing of this book. Even as I continue to write, I find myself searching my heart, repenting and then moving forward into greater understanding of His love for me. I was an idolater and did not know it. As I stated in the introduction, my heart is for the Lord to open our hearts, including mine, and to reveal any hidden areas of darkness where He desires to bring forth light so that we can win the battle against Mammon.

If you are being challenged with economic recession and economic depression and it is adversely affecting you with *depression*—spiritually, mentally and physically—and your relationship with God is in *recession,* then you need this book. And if you have been challenged with these symptoms, it is highly probable that you are struggling with some form of idolatry toward money, wealth and riches. Dear believer, hear me. You are *not* alone in this.

Now is the season when God is bringing attention to money and its form of idolatry. As together we learn more about the spirit of Mammon, the false belief system of Babylon and its idolatry, let us keep our eyes on the prize. God's intent is for you to understand the evil, repent for your involvement with it and then become properly positioned for your inheritance and blessing, for indeed this is His greatest plan for each of us.

Surrender Your Mind and Heart in Prayer

As we begin to examine the ungodly spirit of Mammon, I encourage you to allow your mind and heart to be totally surrendered to the Holy Spirit so that He can reveal His complete truth to you. In fact, I ask you right now to lay your hands on your head and pray this prayer with me:

Father, You have said that I have the mind of Christ. I receive Your mind right now. Open the eyes of my heart so that I may receive truth concerning money, wealth and riches. I repent in advance for any ties to the Babylonian system. Since Babylon means "confusion," I declare that I will not become confused but rather fixed and focused on You and Your Word. I want to be properly positioned and am determined to be blessed and rid of any idolatrous involvement with Mammon. In Jesus' name, Amen.

He will speak if you will listen. Keep your mind set on Him, and He will reveal His truths to you.

The Lord has waited for you to come forth for such a time as this! The same anointing that enabled Esther to face an ancient Babylonian system, break down a death structure and release great wealth to her family and her nation is upon you. You will become empowered by the Holy Spirit to help others break out of bondage and slavery to debt and despair as you lead others to repentance. You will challenge the spirit of Babylon and become a prosperous testimony for His glory. Get ready for a breakthrough and a shift—all for His glory and His Kingdom!

Mammon: The False God of Money

According to the *American Dictionary of the English Language*, mammon is defined as "riches; wealth; or the *god* of riches" (emphasis added).[1] Mammon, therefore, can refer to riches and wealth but also to a false god.

Regarding Matthew 6:24, theologian Albert Barnes writes that Mammon is a Syriac name given to an idol worshiped as the god of riches. It has the same meaning as *Plutus* among the Greeks. It is not known whether or not the Jews ever formally worshiped this idol, but they clearly used the word to denote wealth. The meaning of the passage in Matthew is that one cannot serve the true God and at the same time be supremely engaged in obtaining the riches of this world. This concept is reiterated in Luke 16:9–11: One must interfere with the other.[2]

Another reference, *The Bible Illustrator*, says this concerning Mammon and its unrighteousness:

> Mammon is the name of a Syrian god who presided over wealth. Mammon of unrighteousness means the god whom the unrighteous worship: wealth. It is not necessarily gold, but any wealth—wealth being weal or well-being. Time, talents, opportunity and authority—all are wealth. Here the steward had influence. It is called the Mammon of unrighteousness because it is ordinarily used, not well,

but ill. Power corrupts men. Riches harden more than misfortune.[3]

Mammon, then, is the name of a false god that becomes an idol even to believers if we bow down to it. Remember that Jesus instructed us not to *serve* Mammon. To *serve* a thing indicates that it is a being, that it has a personhood. Indeed, Mammon is a god, and to serve him is to serve Satan! When we serve Mammon, we are worshiping a false god (the devil), and this is idolatry.

Bowing Down to a False Image

Scripture speaks repeatedly about the evil process of "bowing down" to any god other than Jehovah. Careful observation of Exodus 20:4–6 reveals the heart of God concerning idolatry:

> Thou shalt not make unto thee a *graven image*, nor any likeness of any thing that is in heaven above, or that is in the earth beneath, or that is in the water under the earth. Thou shalt *not bow down* thyself unto them, nor serve them, for I Jehovah thy God am a jealous God, visiting the iniquity of the fathers upon the children, upon the third and upon the fourth generation of them that hate me, and showing lovingkindness unto thousands of them that love me and keep my commandments.
>
> ASV, emphasis added

A *graven image* is a carved idol. God allows *no* carvings of any god; to do so would be to create a false god. God is instructing man not to make any false god or to bow down and serve a false god.

Dear ones, the enemy wants our belief systems to become twisted and distorted. If he can pervert our attitudes and belief systems concerning money, riches and wealth, then he can keep us in bondage. Satan makes every attempt to cause us to depend upon money to meet our needs rather than trusting God to be our Provider. If we do not believe that God is able to meet our daily needs, then we are "bowing down" to a false image concerning God! Any image we have of Him that is distorted and untrue is a false image.

To what or whom are you bowing down? You might be reading this first chapter and thinking, *I do not bow down to an idol. I do not serve a false god.*

Bowing down means giving reverence to another being, or giving that being a place of superiority in our lives. In other words, if we listen to the voice of the enemy concerning money and provision and we honor that lie over the truth of what the Lord says concerning His ability to provide for us, then we are basically bowing down to the enemy. If we exalt the lies of Satan over God's Word, then we are bowing down to a false image. If we "imagine" (have an image in our mind) that God does not really care if we are able to pay our bills or that He will not bless our tithes and offerings, then we have a false image of God. If we believe that lie, then we are bowing down to a false image.

I encourage you now to examine your life. What iniquitous patterns are paralyzing you? Are you remaining in captivity because of your iniquitous pattern of bowing down to idols in your life? What are those idols?

If Only I Had a Million Dollars

I have heard Christians say, "If only I had a million dollars, I would . . ."

1. *Give above and beyond my tithe.*

This goal in and of itself is not wrong, but rather is admirable and godly. It is the follow-through that is difficult. I have prayed for Christians to receive financial breakthroughs. Often when it has happened and large amounts of money entered their bank accounts, they have left the church. A spirit of Mammon caught hold of their hearts and corrupted their minds concerning ministry. Overnight the most faithful and productive members of our congregation were seduced and defiled. Their money became their god, and this opened the door for Mammon to speak into their lives concerning their "spiritual direction."

2. *Fund the entire building project.*

Again, this is an admirable plan. But I am embarrassed to admit how many times people who are due for an inheritance have asked me to pray for the release of great wealth to them. I have often felt as if I were being asked to pray for someone's relative to die so that an inheritance would come to them. Of course, the words attached to the plea for prayer were usually something like, "You know, if the funds come, then I can pay for the entire building project. . . . I could completely fund the new wing for the children's church. . . . Our church would really grow with a million-dollar addition!" The spirit of Mammon attempted to seduce me to pray for a "quick release" of money that was really a "sudden death" to a family member. Ouch! Instead I have chosen to pray specifically for the family and for God's perfect will to be accomplished.

And often, when the family member did die, the couple who promised to fund the building addition left the church. Just as soon as the money was released they had "heard from God" that we did not need that new addition. So they left. This is how Mammon perverts God's will concerning money.

3. *Buy a baptismal tank to baptize new believers.*

A baptismal tank (or font, as some congregations call it) is a necessity for any congregation of believers, particularly if your church building is not near a body of water such as a lake, river or ocean. When we first began our church, we needed a portable tank to use until we built our new building. Many prayers went forth concerning this need. One day a businessman came for counsel and prayer. He was praying for a certain real estate investment and was having problems with the closing. "If you will stand with me and believe for this breakthrough, then I will donate a million dollars to this ministry, and you can buy your baptismal tank." Well, we prayed—not for the million dollars, but for his success. We prayed, the elders prayed—we prayed more, the elders prayed more. Prophets ministered to him prophetically and warned him that the enemy had set up a trap. They warned him to guard his heart. They did not know his situation, but God did! The Lord was warning him that Mammon would attempt to make him waver concerning his commitment to the local church in tithes and offerings. Guess what happened? The businessman received millions. The day the property closed he called and said he was on the way with a check. We never saw him again.

4. *Pay off the building note and allow the church to become debt-free.*

I have even heard seasoned ministers say this. One minister I know personally prayed for a long time for a financial breakthrough and finally received over a million dollars for his church. But while he had been believing for that breakthrough, he had developed a lust for money. Yes, his need turned into total lust. The lust went rampant in every way. He started using some of the church's money to buy drugs, and then he used it to buy prostitutes. He soon left the church—taking the money with him. We worked for months ministering to the congregation that had been so wounded and defiled by the lust for money. So you see, Mammon attaches itself to church leaders as well as parishioners. We all are vulnerable to this evil spirit.

Let me again make it clear that there is nothing wrong with desiring to do good things for God's Kingdom with the money He gives you. In fact, God wants our hearts to desire all of these things. When He does give us money, He is honored and blessed when we choose to give above and beyond our tithes, fund church building projects, buy baptismal tanks, pay off building notes, give to missions organizations and more. All of these acts are building the Kingdom of heaven, and God certainly wants us to use our prosperity to fulfill our purpose in Him, to promote His Kingdom and to bless others. But my point is that when people have a lot of money, it seems more difficult to give large sums in tithes. That is the influence of Mammon.

Where Is Our Security?

If we are living in uncertain times, it is easy to worry about money. We might think, *If I had a million dollars, then I would feel secure. I would not have to worry about money anymore.* When we think this way, we are allowing an ungodly fear of not having enough overtake us, and instead of giving, we become more greedy.

Those of us approaching sixty years old can relate to this feeling. We have depended upon a good, stable economy and healthy 401(k)s to provide for our monthly incomes as we head toward retirement. But what are we to do in this present economic crisis? Are we to look for more ways to make money? Perhaps—if God leads us in that direction. But this should not be our focus. Rather, our focus should be on trusting God and seeking His direction for our lives.

If we have ever given in to fear—whether it be fear concerning the future, fear of not investing wisely so that we do not even invest at all, fear that God will not provide or any other fear related to money—then (take a deep breath and get ready to swallow this big pill that will bring later freedom) we have bowed down to an idol. Yes, if we have given in to such fears, then we have worshiped a false image of God. We have trusted in money, wealth and riches rather than God. We have not believed His Word that says, "He has given food and provision to those who reverently and worshipfully fear Him; He will remember His covenant forever and imprint it [on His mind]" (Psalm 111:5, AMP).

We are being seduced daily by Mammon, which causes us to doubt God's Word and to doubt that He desires to bless and prosper us. Out of fear we neglect our tithes and close our pocketbooks, rather than giving joyously. We do not invest money any longer because we are afraid God will not multiply it. We fearfully cower in our time of need. The evil spirit of Mammon overshadows us in our time of desperation.

We need to stop fretting about our economy and remember who our Provider is. The Lord says He is our Provider—why not trust Him?

Serving God or Mammon

Let's turn our focus once again to the topic of serving. We need to take a closer look at what Jesus said in Matthew 6:24:

> No one can serve two masters; for either he will hate the one and love the other, or he will stand by and be devoted to the one and despise and be against the other. You cannot serve God and mammon (deceitful riches, money, possessions, or whatever is trusted in).
>
> AMP

In the New Testament Greek, the word for *serve* is *douleuo*, which implies being a slave to another.[4] Jesus was making it clear that when we choose God, we also serve Him. If we choose to bow down to a false image, then we serve that false god.

In the Old Testament, Joshua instructed Israel to choose so that they would also serve: "*Choose* you this day whom ye will *serve*" (Joshua 24:15, KJV, emphasis added). Joshua was referring to Israel's choice to serve false gods or the Lord. In the Promised Land was the wealth and breakthrough God had prophesied and promised. Israel had to decide whether they were going to choose the Lord, who would then bless them with His promises, or idols, who offered nothing but sure death. Notice that Israel's choice did not have anything to do with whether or not God desired to bless them; their choice was simply which god they would *serve*. We are faced with the same choice today: Will we serve Mammon or the Lord?

When Joshua presented Israel with this choice, he was referring to both worship and servitude. His question was whether they would worship God or false gods or serve

God or false gods. The Hebrew word for *serve, abad*, refers not only to being a worshiper but also to a bond-service relationship. Being a bond servant means that one is bound by choice to another, giving complete dedication and servitude to that relationship.[5]

Both of these Scriptures indicate that two masters are involved: God and Mammon. When we choose to serve one of them, that one becomes master over us. Choosing to serve God allows Him to be our master. Submitting to and serving Mammon, on the other hand, allows him to become master over us—and results in a spirit of bondage.

The Spirit of Bondage

> For ye have not received the spirit of bondage again to fear; but ye have received the Spirit of adoption, whereby we cry, Abba, Father.
>
> Romans 8:15, KJV

In their insightful book *Strongman's His Name . . . What's His Game?* Carol and Jerry Robeson look at various biblical references to the spirit of bondage and describe the *spirit of bondage* as:

Fears (see Romans 8:15)

Addictions (see Romans 8:15; 2 Peter 2:19)

Fear of death (see Hebrews 2:14–15)

Captivity to Satan (see 2 Peter 2:19)

Servant of corruption (see Luke 8:26–29; John 8:34; Acts 8:23; Romans 6:16; 7:23)

Compulsive sin (see Proverbs 5:22; John 8:34)

Bondage to sin (see 2 Timothy 2:26)[6]

36

When I began to study the Robesons' list of manifestations of a spirit of bondage, I personally identified with a generational stronghold of fear. I began to observe the ways in which my generation viewed money, and I quickly identified a fear of losing money, a poverty mentality and a belief that "if we just had a lot of money all our problems would be solved." Hoarding money seemed to be the family cure-all for crisis. To believe that money is the ultimate Band-aid is idolatry. A belief system with that type of foundation is one built upon idolatry and Mammon.

We saw in Matthew 6:24 that Jesus warned the disciples about bondage to Mammon. He connected it with serving either God or Mammon. Let's look at this verse again: "No one can serve two masters. Either he will hate the one and love the other, or he will be devoted to the one and despise the other. You cannot serve both God and Money."

In this passage Jesus warns about love versus hate. He is basically telling us that we cannot allow money to master us. When money masters us, servanthood is required. Furthermore, if we serve money, then we "hate" God! If we serve God, on the other hand, then we become His servants and "hate" Mammon. Money itself is neutral. It is the worshiping of it that is evil. Jesus is stating that we cannot be devoted to both at the same time. Jesus further instructs us that it is absolutely impossible to be devoted to money and ungodly wealth (a type of bowing down to Mammon) and at the same time to be devoted to God.

He goes on further and connects money to worry:

Therefore I tell you, do not worry about your life, what you will eat or drink; or about your body, what you will wear. Is not life more important than food, and the body more important than clothes? Look at the birds of the air;

they do not sow or reap or store away in barns, and yet your heavenly Father feeds them. Are you not much more valuable than they? Who of you by worrying can add a single hour to his life?

Matthew 6:25–27

I have personally worried over money. Many of you have worried over money. Jesus said that we cannot add any extra time to our lives by worrying. This tells me that if we worry, a death structure begins to be built around us. What I mean is that worry robs us of life! *Strong's* defines *worry* as "anxiety and distraction." It is rooted in the word *merizo*, which means "disunite, differ and divide."[7] When we worry over money we become anxious. Anxiety is a form of fear, and fear is bondage. Worry, then, is a form of bondage. Are you beginning to understand how Mammon works? We become bond servants of Mammon when we are fearful concerning a lack of money. If we worry, then we are not agreeing with God's Word and His promises concerning His desire to care for us. According to the interpretation in *Strong's*, we "disunite (from being in unity with God's Word), differ (or become argumentative and resistant) and (become) divided."[8] If we are divided in our thoughts concerning God's ability to care for us, then we are double-minded and unstable in all our ways (see James 1:8).

Jesus comforts us by instructing us not to worry even about our clothes:

And why do you worry about clothes? See how the lilies of the field grow. They do not labor or spin. Yet I tell you that not even Solomon in all his splendor was dressed like one of these. If that is how God clothes the grass of the field, which is here today and tomorrow is thrown into the fire, will he not much more clothe you, O you of little faith? So do not worry, saying, "What shall we eat?" or "What shall we drink?" or "What shall we wear?" For the *pagans* run after all these things, and your heavenly Father knows that you need them. But seek first his kingdom and his righteousness, and all these things will be given to you as well. Therefore do not worry about tomorrow, for tomorrow will worry about itself. Each day has enough trouble of its own.

Matthew 6:28–34, emphasis added

Notice that Jesus says "pagans" run after the material things in life. Pagans are idol worshipers.

I do not have enough room in this chapter to explain how much I love clothes and how much I fret over wearing the right clothing when I travel and minister. It gets ridiculous. And I now recognize this as sin, for it is serving Mammon. *I repent, Lord. When I fret over these things, I am being divided and double-minded. Worry is stealing my life and joy. I do not want to be like the pagans and run after the material things. I choose this day to worship only You. I will be anxious for nothing.*

Bondage is a lack of liberty. God says that He wants us "free indeed" (see John 8:36). The Greek word for "indeed" is *ontos*, which refers to knowing with certainty the truth, but it is also rooted in a word that refers to understanding the truth of "who you are" and that you are created in God's divine image.[9] The main problem with us as believers is that we do not truly know *who* we are and *whose* we are! Sometimes it is more an image problem than a Mammon problem. In fact, many times the image problem opens the door to a Mammon problem.

Dear ones, do I have your attention yet? I surely pray so. If you are being convicted of any bondage at all, including being a slave to the past, then it is time to look further at your belief system concerning money.

Consider Your Life

Before we continue on our journey together and allow the Lord to expose the spirit of Mammon further, I encourage you to consider whether or not any area of your life has placed you in bondage to Mammon. Do you fear, for example, that if you tithe you will not be able to pay your bills? If you realize that specific fear has brought great torment, then you may be bowing down to Mammon. The result is idolatry. Maybe an addiction has developed and you are in tremendous bondage. Is it possible that you have attempted to be free, yet you are continually trapped due to the stronghold of Mammon? We can overspend and be in debt because we are addicted to "stuff." We charge enormous amounts to credit cards for instant gratification rather than seeking God for complete fulfillment. Dear ones, this is an anointed time to take these concerns to the Lord and repent. Let's do that, shall we?

Write below any areas where you can identify with the spirit of bondage.

1. _____

2. _____

3. _____

4. _____

5. _____

When we repent, we are asking for forgiveness for a specific sin, and then we choose to turn away from the sin and run back to God. True repentance leads to a change in our belief systems and lifestyles. Repentance places us in right standing with the Father. I encourage you to write in the space below your prayer of repentance for allowing yourself to bow down to fear, worrying about money and allowing a door to be open to Mammon.

_____

_____

_____

_____

_____

_____

_____

_____

Now please give me the privilege of praying for you:

Father, I lift up each person reading this book and ask that You open his or her eyes to truth. Your truth will set each of us free. Empower each reader as he or she repents from any involvement with the enemy, especially concerning Mammon. I ask that You strengthen Your child each day to serve only You. Be with Your child as he or she completes this book and renews his or her mind to Your divine will. In Jesus' name, Amen.

Dear ones, it is time to be free indeed. Now position yourself for a great breakthrough in God!

2

Babylon and Wealth

Fallen! Fallen is Babylon the Great!

Revelation 18:2

A firm biblical foundation makes it clear that we must not bow down to idolatry and helps us to understand why Mammon and Babylon are a threat to Christianity. As we move further into our study and establishing this biblical foundation, we must take time to study symbolism.

Most of us are aware that Scripture is packed full of symbols, types, shadows and signs. Babylon is one of these types that symbolizes the world system. Babylon is mentioned in both the Old and New Testaments. In the book of Revelation, all references to Babylon are likely symbolic. Revelation 14:8, for instance, describes Babylon as "Babylon the Great," and is referring to the spirit of the world committing spiritual adultery against God. Revelation 17:5 speaks of Babylon's name, which is written on her forehead: "Mystery, Babylon the Great, The Mother of Prostitutes and of the Abominations of the Earth."

Another alarming symbol of Babylon is found in Revelation 18, which speaks of God's declaration to destroy Babylon because she is a home for demons:

> Fallen! Fallen is Babylon the Great!
> She has become a home for demons
> and a haunt for every evil spirit.
>
> Revelation 18:2

Babylon has nothing but evil attachments, and the Babylonian world system is detestable to God. Indeed, He promises to destroy it. The sad thing is that we are born into this demonic system, and it is familiar to us. It is difficult to be on guard against such an evil when we have embraced it for most of our lives.

As I stated earlier, money is neutral, but the love of money is addictive and imprisons us, making us captive to Satan. Through love of money and power, Satan seduces our values and seeks to ensnare us into compromising our trust and faith in God. If we *buy into* (pun intended) the system of Babylon, embracing its idolatry, whoredoms and evil, then we become prey to a "destroyer spirit" that seeks to devour us.

The Destroyer Spirit

The destroyer spirit is mentioned several times in the Bible, both in the Hebrew (Old Testament) and Greek (New Testament). The first is in the book of Exodus. Right before Israel was released from captivity, "the destroyer" killed the firstborn in Egypt (see Exodus 12:23). At God's command, the children of Israel placed lambs' blood on their doorposts, and the destroyer spirit passed over their homes. Therefore, the spirit of death had no "open door" to enter and destroy where the blood of the lamb was displayed. Saints, in the same way today the destroyer spirit is looking for an open door into our lives. We must plead the blood of the Lamb, Jesus, over the doorposts of our hearts. Only then can we be freed to come out of Egypt—that is, the Babylonian system that attempts to destroy us. If we do not, then the destroyer has an open door into our lives.

The final mention of the destroyer is found in Revelation 9:11: "They have a king ruling over them, who is the angel in charge of the abyss. His name in Hebrew is Abaddon; in Greek the name is Apollyon (meaning 'The Destroyer')" (GNT).

The destroyer's function is simple: to destroy and bring death to all that God loves—and that includes us as believers. In addition, the destroyer desires to annihilate our belief in God's desire to bless us. This is why we are easily seduced into believing that the world system is our source, therefore committing idolatry. The destroyer is relentless in his seductions to worship him and trust him over God. If we come into covenant with his lies, then we are destroyed.

To escape falling prey to the destroyer spirit and to possess the future God has for us, we must shift out of the world system of Babylon. In other words, we must "come out" of Babylon and its evil seductions and completely give our hearts to God.

Coming Out of Babylon

Babylonian thinking is a system of false beliefs concerning provision. We fall into this belief system by becoming ensnared by the lies and seductions of the destroyer. One way to come out of this belief system is to trust God and His Word.

According to 1 Corinthians 10:10, the destroyer has an open door to attack us if we murmur and complain. While in the wilderness, the Israelites murmured against God and Moses concerning provision (see Numbers 14). We are doing the same thing when we murmur against God concerning our finances.

Murmuring and complaining are a big deal to God. The biblical concept of murmuring is much more than a slight complaint or a mere side-mouthed grumble. The word *murmur* comes from the Hebrew word *luwn* and implies someone stopping, lodging, dwelling or staying permanently in a bad place (maybe emotional or spiritual). When we murmur and complain, therefore, we stop and remain in a destructive place or pattern of behavior. Did you get that? When we murmur against God concerning our provision, we actually are stopping permanently in our forward advancement in Him and actually living in the camp of the enemy. Dare I go on? Beloved, when we murmur we are in prideful rebellion against God and His perfect plan for us.

The way to "come out" is to trust God completely for our daily bread and provision. Only in trusting Him are we able to overthrow the Babylonian system.

Tithing and Giving

Part of trusting God for our daily bread involves our heart attitudes toward tithing and giving. If our hearts are not in line with God's Word, then we fall prey to the system of Babylon. We are at our most vulnerable during times of economic crisis, when the destroyer spirit strikes its hardest and tempts us to withdraw from giving as God commands.

Let me assure you that the spirit of Mammon does not want you monetarily blessing God's Kingdom. Yet Malachi states that we are robbing God if we withhold our tithes and offerings. At the risk of sounding legalistic, which I am not at all, please take a close look at what the Lord says concerning tithes and offerings:

> Will a man rob God? Yet you are robbing Me! But you say, "How have we robbed You?" In tithes and offerings. You are cursed with a curse. . . . Bring the whole tithe into the storehouse . . . and test Me now in this. . . . (See) if I will not open for you the windows of heaven and pour out for you a blessing until it overflows. Then I will rebuke the *devourer* for you, so that it will not *destroy* the fruits of the ground; nor will your vine in the field cast its grapes. . . . All the nations will call you blessed, for you shall be a delightful land. . . . Your words have been *arrogant* against Me. . . . Yet you say, "What have we spoken against You?" *You have said, "It is vain to serve God*; and what profit is it that we have kept His charge?"
>
> Malachi 3:8–14 (NASB, emphasis added)

This passage exposes the destroyer, as well as a curse that overshadows us if we are prideful and serve Mammon instead of God. If we rebelliously believe we have a better plan than what God has decreed and established, then we will be unfruitful. Withholding from God (hoarding) due to fear of lack opens the door to the destroyer, who desires to destroy our fruit. Again, I am not attempting to bring condemnation; rather, I want to offer avenues out of bondage to Mammon.

How often do we complain because others appear to be blessed more than we are? The passage in Malachi points to the murmurings of our hearts: "It is vain to serve God. I cannot see the profit in it. Others in the world are blessed, yet I serve God and am suffering lack" (verses 14–15, paraphrased). Friends, when we complain in our hearts in this way, we are coming into agreement with the seductions of Mammon and Babylon. We are agreeing with Satan's voice. We must therefore remain on guard.

The key to being financially prosperous is tithing and giving, and the Architect who designed the blueprint for our future knows what is "best for becoming blessed." If we give God what is already His, then He will "open for [us] the windows of heaven and pour out for [us] a blessing until it overflows" (Malachi 3:10, NASB). And He promises to rebuke the devourer and not allow the destroyer to rob His planned blessings.

We must be alert against the cunning devices of our enemy, the destroyer, who is an angel of death. If we maintain a poverty mentality and murmur against God, then a death structure is erected about us.

What is a death structure? In my recent book, *Strategies from Heaven's Throne*, I state:

> Whatever is not releasing life must be recognized as possibly releasing death, so we call these "death structures." Webster's Dictionary defines *structure* as "the manner

48

of which something is constructed, as a building." . . . It implies how something is built.[1]

A structure implies a framework of some type—how our belief systems are framed, for example. God has a framework (structure) for our lives that will always release life, and Satan has a plan that always results in death. If we believe Satan over God, then the enemy has legal permission to spin a web of death about us. Being in agreement with the devil opens the door to the destroyer.

We must therefore keep the doorposts of our hearts guarded and not allow the destroyer to enter with his lies and deceit. Examining our attitudes toward tithing and giving is an important factor in coming out of Babylonian thinking.

Babylon: The Kingdom of Satan

To understand how we have been seduced by the system of Babylon, we must look first at the foundations of Babylon itself. The ancient kingdom of Babylon began with Nimrod, the son of Cush, who was a son of Ham and grandson of Noah. He was a great man in his day and a mighty hunter, and the heart of his empire included *Babel* (the Hebrew word for *Babylon*) (see Genesis 10:8–10).

As a great hunter Nimrod gathered men under his command. The more skilled he became, the more others followed until he actually made himself "master of the country and brought them under subjection."[2] Being a mighty hunter, however, seemed minute compared to building kingdoms.

Nimrod became a great builder, and he most likely was the architect of the Tower of Babel. Under his supervision the tower was constructed, and the beginning of Babylon was established. One might wonder if Nimrod had the primitive skyscraper constructed out of his own oppression and violent defiance against God, daring heaven even as each brick was placed. Whether it was the people who built the tower to "be like God" or Nimrod himself who laid the foundations of monarchy, we must recognize that Nimrod was a man of great ambition and authority.

Nimrod's desire to lord over others and build great kingdoms out of selfish ambition laid strong foundations within the kingdom of Babylon. The false religion he established became a cult and opened the door to more idolatry. The proud spirit behind this type of foundation is like Lucifer (see Isaiah 14:14–15), who consistently seeks to be exalted above God. Indeed, Nimrod laid a foundation of selfish ambition that would support death structures for thousands of years to come.

My friend, author Jane Hamon, wrote the following in her insightful book:

> The foundations of Babylon were established in the first book of the Bible, Genesis, chapter eleven, when people set their hearts in rebellion against God and began to build a tower to heaven. . . . From beginning to end in the Word of God we find the city of Babylon is a representation of a system of false religion, full of idolatry, false authority, founded in rebellion; and systems of false government, established through unrighteous gain and underwritten by the monetary systems of the world.[3]

Nimrod worshiped himself, rather than God. His aspirations for greatness, eminence and building his own kingdom set him in opposition with the King of kings and His Kingdom. As he set up a new government and religion within his territories, Nimrod fueled idolatry, which became foundational for the future Babylonian system. It is a system that is still active today under the authority of Satan, and it has the same effect today—selfish ambition, pride and idolatry. The kingdom of Babylon is a kingdom that is totally opposite of God's Kingdom. It opposes God, His Word and all prophetic declarations concerning future provision. It represents all that is false and evil. It is advanced by the same demonic spirit of pride that influenced Nimrod to exalt himself above God.

Theologian Matthew Henry comments on the pride of Nimrod by stating, "He thought himself a mighty prince, but before the Lord (that is, in God's account) he was but a mighty hunter. Note: Great conquerors are but great hunters."[4] In the same way, Satan attempts to hunt us down as prey and to conquer us. He does indeed prowl around as a roaring lion, seeking whom he can destroy (see 1 Peter 5:8–9).

We face widespread idolatry today on a daily basis as we battle against the demonic Babylonian world system. Our world trade, world markets and monetary systems are defiled by the spirit of idolatry, as many of us trust money over God's promises. Choosing to resist the lies of Satan and to stand firm in the faith is another key to coming out of Babylon.

Saints, let's make this choice! It is our season to overthrow the evil behind our economy and personal belief systems concerning money.

Ammon Re: The False God of Nimrod and the "Gate of God"

In order to better understand Nimrod's Babylonian system, we must delve further into the religion of this pagan king. Nimrod was a Cushite out of Africa (Ethiopia). *Fausset's*

Bible Dictionary points out the significance of studying the national god of the Cushites, for it will help us to understand the idolatrous basis of the worldly Babylonian system that operates today.[5]

Fausset's states that Nimrod himself named Babylon "The Gate of Gods" or simply "The Gate of God."[6] (Later the word *Babylon* also was translated to mean "confusion.") He named his city, then, after the god whom he worshiped.

Nimrod's primary idol, Mammon, was named after the Cushite god *Ammon Re*, whose name means "hidden." Also known as *Ra* in Egypt, this idol was considered the father of all gods, meaning that he was the creator of every human being and all creatures. He was worshiped because of his connection to reproduction and was represented by a ram. Since his name means "hidden," this idol is strongly connected to the occult, "those things which are hidden and concealed."[7]

The system of Babylon was based upon a false idol, Mammon. Our entire world economy, therefore, is rooted in a false and evil god. Can we not see, then, how the foundations of our world system became so defiled? Any time we exalt *anything* above God it is idolatry—especially when we exalt money. And if on a personal basis we have any roots in the world system, namely the love of money, are we not also defiled?

Dear ones, the veil that has masked Mammon and Babylon has lifted. It is time for revelation and war against our enemy. How can God trust His children with more money when they belong to the world system? This is a question we need to consider seriously.

Today's economy leaves no room for ignorance—especially spiritual! We cannot serve both God and Mammon. We cannot serve God's Kingdom and Satan's kingdom.

Jesus referred to the Jews as "an adulterous generation" because they would not shift into present truth. We, too, are adulterers if we resist present truth and revelation. Let me continue to be blunt. If we bow down to money, we are committing idolatry. But dear believers, if we can tear down idolatry, then we can also unlock our harvest!

The key to the releasing of godly wealth is to repent for idolatry and embrace truth. If we will repent and *turn,* then we will experience a mighty harvest and transference of wealth from the world system to the Kingdom of God.

Idolatry Builds a Throne

Idol worship builds a throne of Satan, referred to in Scripture as "Satan's seat" (Revelation 2:13, KJV). My good friend and prophetic author Chuck Pierce validates the simple fact that the corporate sin of idolatry builds a foundation for the throne of Satan:

> Satan's assigned hierarchy rules from a throne built on the corporate iniquity of a region, and his throne is linked with the worship in that area. Remember: Satan wanted to exalt himself to become like God so that he would be worshiped. Satan continues to exalt himself, attempting to draw all people to his counterfeit light. . . . All iniquity on earth is actually working from a satanic system of worship meant to usurp God's authority and keep lost souls in darkness to the truth of the Gospel.[8]

The worship of Mammon in ancient Babylon laid the foundation for the Babylonian system and built a seat for Satan. This demonic stronghold is still in power today, and this is why we are still enslaved to Mammon. Idolatry disrupts God's original intent to bless us and gives Satan an upper hand to destroy us. When we keep Satan on that throne, when our trust is in money rather than God, we are simply continuing in an idolatrous pattern.

The City of Shinar

Babel was the capital of the country called Shinar in the book of Genesis. (Later in Scripture, it is called Chaldea.) We learn more about the country of Shinar in the account of Abraham and Lot.

When Abraham and his nephew, Lot, separated, Abraham allowed Lot to choose which land he wanted. Lot chose the choicest, most lush and fruitful land, Sodom and Gomorrah, as his home. Not long after, a confederacy of kings came against Sodom and Gomorrah and overtook them, capturing and enslaving Lot and his family. The King of Shinar, or Babylon, was one of the kings in this confederacy. So we can actually conclude that a spirit of Babylon stole Lot, his family and his possessions. Why? When Lot chose Sodom and Gomorrah, he willfully submitted to a sinful and defiled country and its government. In doing so, he opened the door to an evil spirit and to future captivity by Babylon. In the same way that Lot's choices opened such a door, our choices for worldly pleasures place us in bondage to Babylonian captivity. If we submit to the Babylonian system, then we become slaves to it.

Abraham was a Hebrew, a name that translates "one who crossed over."[9] Abraham had to put on his warfare mantle and "cross over" to rescue his family from slav-

ery to Babylonian kings. I believe that we as believers
will have to war over our future blessing to "cross over"
into our Promised Land. This is not a season to remain
passive. Many blessings await us, but first we will have
to battle against Mammon and Babylon and repent for
wrong choices.

Furthermore, the name of the King of Shinar was Amraphel. I point out in my recent book, *Strategies from
Heaven's Throne: Claiming the Life God Wants for You,*
that the name *Amraphel* means "sayer of darkness."[10]
Believers, Babylon speaks only darkness and defeat! The
strategy behind this evil spirit is to speak darkness over
every situation. When the devil speaks over our futures,
his words are always seductive and hopeless.

We could easily respond to God in fear, doubt and failure. But instead, we must stand, resist and have faith in
Him. We must be careful whose spirit we heed. Rather than
bowing down to the dark sayings of Satan, we must choose
to obey only the Holy Spirit and His Word over us.

In the same book I wrote:

> There will never be any hope in [Amraphel's] words.
> Most of us are at war against the evil effects of the
> Babylonian spirit. The stronghold is like an octopus,
> wrapping its demonic tentacles around businesses, cor-
> porations, governments, school systems, churches and
> families. Not only does the spirit pervert the economic
> system, but it also demonically influences structures and
> governments.[11]

Let's face it. Our generations have bowed their knee to
Mammon. We must be like Abraham and cross over to
fight for our future generations to be freed from bondage
and slavery to the enemy.

The Importance of Gates

I mentioned that Nimrod named Babylon, which means "The Gate of God." A gate is also a door of entrance.

In the ancient world, gates were the main entrances into cities. But during battle they were also the most vulnerable places, for once an enemy penetrated the gate, he could ransack the city. To possess the gate was to possess the city. Gates were therefore heavily defended to protect the city.

When the Canaanites erected a city gate, their religious practice was to offer up a human sacrifice to their false gods. They believed that a blood sacrifice to their idols would provide that gate with supernatural protection from their enemies. A blood sacrifice supposedly guaranteed protection.

Gates were also the places where trade took place. The market area was normally right next to the gated entrance, and villagers, as well as traders from other parts of the world, brought produce and goods to sell. Imagine the competition at the gates each day. Since there was no refrigeration, there was a tremendous need for fresh food, so the market was open every weekday (see Nehemiah 10:31).

Public meetings and civil government also were established at the gates. Judges met and conversed there (see Proverbs 1:21; 2 Chronicles 32:6; Jeremiah 17:19; Ruth 4:1–2).

So gates were more than merely entrances or exits. We see that taking a gate meant taking a city, and government was established at the gates of a city. When the gates were dedicated to idols with a blood sacrifice, then the city and government would therefore be Satan's kingdom.

Babylon was known as the "city of gates," for it was surrounded by one hundred brass gates. Each of these gates was erected in pagan worship, and each was named for a false god. The gate of Samas, the gate of Zagaga and the gate of Enlil are several examples. Samas was worshiped as the sun god, Zagaga was worshiped as one of the gods of war, and Enlil was worshiped as the greatest of gods—the god over all the earth. So the main gates surrounding the perimeters of Babylon were all dedicated to devils and idols.

Even the streets connected to the gates bore the names of idols:

> According to an Assyrian and a Babylonian list of gates, the streets bore names connected with those of the gates to which they led. Thus, the street of the gate of Zagaga, one of the gods of war, was called "the street of Zagaga, who expels his enemies"; that of the gate of Merodach was "the street of Merodach, shepherd of his land"; while the street of Ishtar's gate was "the street of Ishtar, patron of her people." The city-gates named after Enlil, Addu (Hadad or Rimmon), Samas the Sun-god, Sin the Moon-god, etc., had streets similarly indicated.[12]

Thus, because of the idolatrous worship and sacrifices at its gates of entrance, the city of Babylon became Satan's kingdom and dominion.

Go through the Gates

In the same way that the gates of Babylon opened the way for the city to become Satan's dominion, we erect spiritual gates for him today. This is a dynamic that we must understand in order to war effectively against Satan and his world system. Spiritually, we cannot enter into enlargement unless we "go through the gates."

Isaiah made a prophetic declaration to the Jews during their season of captivity: "Go through, go through the gates; prepare ye the way of the people; cast up, cast up the highway; gather out the stones; lift up an ensign for the peoples" (Isaiah 62:10, ASV). Isaiah was telling God's people to go through the gates of Babylon. We must do the same today; that is, we must take the wealth of Babylon through prayer, warfare, repentance and returning to God. We should pray that the world system of Babylon bow its knee to God. In this way we will overthrow Mammon and take back what has been stolen by the enemy. We cannot reap the spoils of the fortress of Babylon, however, unless we are determined to battle at the gates.

Isaiah's prophecy includes a description of a standard being lifted as a covering for the people. Precious believers, Jesus is our standard, and He is our covering. We need not fear the economy, the spirit of Mammon or the spirit of Babylon. God is our source. Look at what else Isaiah prophesies:

> Lift up your *heads*, O ye *gates*; and be ye lift up, ye everlasting *doors*; and the King of glory shall come in. Who is this King of glory? The LORD strong and mighty, the LORD mighty in battle. Lift up your heads, O ye gates; even lift them up, ye everlasting doors; and the King of glory shall come in. Who is this King of glory? The LORD of hosts, he is the King of glory. Selah.
>
> Psalm 24:7–10, KJV, emphasis added

God instructs us to lift up our heads and minds to Him. Our thinking process is a gate of entrance, and He desires to renew our minds. Believers, stand strong! This is our season to arise in great faith because the King of Glory is coming into our circumstances and establishing His Kingdom in our midst. There are doors and gates to our minds, belief systems, lives and hearts—all of which God is protecting, exposing and transforming.

Spiritually, gates are important for they serve as entrances for both good and bad. We don't want to allow the enemy to have an entrance in our lives, so we must know how to "shut that gate." Every time Satan knocks on our door, we must challenge him, resist him and protect our gate of entrance. When we "go through the gates," we destroy the altars of the enemy and take back the city for God.

Nebuchadnezzar's Tower and False God

Nebuchadnezzar also was a king of Babylon and a prideful architect. "Is this not Babylon the great, which *I* myself have built?" (Daniel 4:30, NASB, emphasis added). His pride and idolatrous worship were a main gate of entrance to Satan.

A French expedition uncovered ruins that indicated Nebuchadnezzar rebuilt Babylon when he reigned as king. His temple, or tower of Nebo, stood on the basement of the old tower of Babel. Nebo was an idol of both Babylon and Assyria and was considered to be their "guardian god" and their god of learning, wisdom and education. *Nebo* is also connected to the Hebrew word *nabi*, which means "prophet."

When Nebuchadnezzar set up his tower of Nebo, he included an inscription that said, "The most ancient monument of Babylon I built and finished; I exalted its head with bricks covered with copper . . . the house of the seven lights [the seven planets]; a former king 42 ages ago built, but did not complete its head."

This inscription gives us further insight into the spirits behind today's world system. In erecting his own temple on the Tower of Babel's former foundation, Nebuchadnezzar was attempting to resurrect the idolatry connected to Babel. He dedicated it to his false gods and took pride in the kingdom that "he built." Just as God came down to examine the tower of Babel and then sent confusion to their language, He also judged what Nebuchadnezzar had built and caused Nebuchadnezzar to lose his mind.

Nebuchadnezzar also dedicated temples to "E-mah, the goddess Nin-mah near the Ishtar-gate; a white stone temple for Sin, the Moon-god; E-ditur-kalma, 'the house of the judge of the land,' for Samas, the Sun-god; E-sa-tila, for Gula, the goddess of healing; E–hursag-ella, 'the house of the holy mountain,'" etc. Indeed, Babylon was a city of idols.

Among these temples King Nebuchadnezzar erected a sanctuary called Du-azua, "a place of fate." At each New Year's festival, which occurred on the eighth and ninth of the Hebraic month of Nisan, the "king of the gods of heaven and earth" was honored and the future Babylonian monarchs were declared.[13] This time of year coincides with the end of March and beginning of April on our calendar. Dear ones, Satan still wants this same exalted position today. As long as the devil has a seated position in our economy, during this same time of year a demonic confederacy declares that Satan is still king of Babylon and king over us as well. It is a time when we must watch carefully, guarding our gates, for the enemy wants to destroy us.

At this moment I am writing this chapter in the month of Nisan. I am reminded again to protect every gate, guard every entrance into my mind and heart and resist the enemy who seeks to devour my faith in God and His ability to provide.

The Anointing of Cyrus

God used King Cyrus to release Israel from Babylon and to empower them to return to Israel. He therefore delivered Israel from bondage and oppression. In this way, King Cyrus was a type of Christ. In her book, *The Cyrus Decree*, Jane Hamon says, "Cyrus was a type, or a foreshadow, of the great Deliverer, Jesus Christ, who would come to deliver people out of captivity and lead them into a place of freedom, promise, wealth and blessing."[14] In Isaiah 45:1, the Lord calls Cyrus His "anointed."

Indeed, Christ is the "Anointed One." And through Him, we Christians receive the same anointing and are called to destroy the enemy. Through Christ and His blood we are anointed to be modern day Cyruses who will conquer Babylon, tear down fat foundations of idolatry and Mammon, and rebuild the altars of God in our businesses, economy and culture. If we will set our hearts toward God and allow Him to direct our lives, then we also can be used as God's instruments today.

To overthrow the evil spirits of captivity, we must recognize that the enemy has already been defeated at the cross; yet we must still battle giants in the land. The giants we face are fear, doubt, unbelief, poverty, bondage, idolatry, Mammon, etc. These must be conquered for us to be free.

We also must be determined to go to war and subdue the enemy. Isaiah 45:1 says this concerning Cyrus: "Whose right hand I [God] have held—to subdue nations before him" (NKJV).Cyrus was given a supernatural power to defeat his enemies. The same power is also given to us as believers! Just as Cyrus went to war, and Abraham went to war against Babylon, we must go to war against evil to protect the seeds of generations. There is no room for fear. We must put on a warfare mantle in this season and set our faces as flint toward the possession of our future.

In closing, look at what Isaiah goes on to say about Cyrus. He says that God will open the gates to Babylon for those who have the heart of Cyrus:

> This is Jehovah's message to Cyrus, God's anointed, whom he has chosen to conquer many lands. God shall empower his right hand and he shall crush the strength of mighty kings. God shall open the gates of Babylon to him; the gates shall not be shut against him any more. I will go before you, Cyrus, and level the mountains and smash down the city gates of brass and iron bars. And I will give you treasures hidden in the darkness, secret riches; and you will know that I am doing this—I, the Lord, the God of Israel, the one who calls you by your name.
>
> Isaiah 45:1–3, TLB

Dear one, you have power! Just as God opened the gates of Babylon and gave Cyrus power and riches, He will open the gates of Babylon to you, and you will have victory over your enemy. And you will be given treasures and secret riches that have been hidden in the darkness (see Isaiah 45:3).

A Prayer of Repentance

Now that we have established a firm understanding of the roots of Babylon and the gates of entrance, it is time to stop and pray. Later we will discuss how to completely demolish altars of iniquity, and we will rebuild the altars of God. But before doing those things we must first repent. Repentance is always the first step in destroying any power of darkness.

Father, I come to You in the name of Jesus. I thank You for His shed blood, which makes me righteous in Your eyes. I repent of the sin of . . . (Name each area that the Holy Spirit speaks to you. Take your time because this is important.) I repent especially for the sin of idolatry, fear, love of money, lack of trust in God, murmuring, rebellion and any gates I have opened that have allowed entrance to the enemy. (Ask Him once more if you have opened any gates to the devil.)

Since the sins of the fathers are passed to the third and fourth generations, I ask that You forgive my ancestors for any involvement for the sins I named. I ask You to forgive me for my involvement.

I repent for not protecting my heart and my thoughts concerning Mammon and the spirits behind Babylon.

I am thankful once more for the precious blood of Jesus that cleanses me from all unrighteousness. I apply His blood to the doorpost of my heart, which binds the destroyer and the spirit of death and looses Your blessings into my life and into my generations.

In Jesus' name, Amen.

Good job! I am proud of you for pressing through this chapter. It was a tough one, I know, but much needed. I want to assure you that I daily take you before the Lord and pray for you as you read this book, plus I have a team of intercessors who are praying as I write. God knows exactly what you need and when you need it; don't ever doubt His faithfulness. I want to expose the enemy because I want you to be free—free indeed!

Now, take the hand of the Holy Spirit. Ask Him to lead you into the next chapter. He is near you and desires to lead you into more truth.

3

Iniquity, Tyre and Seats of Authority

> But he shall say, I tell you, I know you
> not whence ye are; depart from me, all ye
> workers of iniquity.
>
> Luke 13:27, KJV

It was the Christmas season in New York. Vacationers, family members, businessmen and women all flocked to the center of corporate America. Unfortunately, this vast multitude significantly slowed down traffic and congested the downtown districts.

Impatiently, Boss peeked through the drapes of his penthouse window. "Where is that limousine? There must be fifty taxis down there, but not the limo I specifically requested for today! The influx of people at this time of year makes it impossible to do business as usual! Don't these people realize we have deadlines and time-crunches?" He scowled as he spoke.

The head of a large corporation in New York, this man was known simply as "Boss" to everyone. He treated others as if he were the only person in the world with a life. While his given name was Christian, he did not like to use it because he believed that in the world of business people equated it with religion and might take him for a corporate pansy.

Faith, Boss's wife of twelve years, went to stand beside her husband at the window. "Honey, I wish you would just take a day off to spend with us. The children are out of school for the holidays. And, please, please don't forget that Hope is in the church Christmas play tonight. It begins at seven—*sharp*."

"Well, I'll . . ."

"Don't say you'll try! I simply cannot go through another Christmas play without your supporting our children. They miss you. You need to spend time with *all* of us. Besides that, you haven't been in church for years. Surely, at Christmastime you can take off just one night! Last year you missed it because you went to Europe to ensure a corporate buyout. Remember?"

Boss stretched his collar and loosened his tie. "Well, somebody has to pay for this penthouse," he countered.

"The penthouse was your idea. I never wanted to live in New York anyway. I hate it here. We have taxis and limos picking up our children for school, for activities, even to drive them to their friends' houses. The only time I am able to drive them anywhere myself is to church on Sunday mornings because the traffic is more manageable then. And we never see you. You don't even get home from work until after we have eaten dinner and the children have said their prayers and are asleep."

"Don't lecture me about your prayer time again. You don't need me here to pray. You seem to be doing a good job all by yourself."

Faith backed off. *Lord, help me! I am at my wits' end here. You have got to intervene. I have been faithful to You and to this marriage, but he is so caught up in success that I can no longer reach him.* Faith continued to silently pray, then headed back into the kitchen. As she passed the refrigerator her eyes caught the inspirational magnet Hope had given her on Mother's Day: "All things are possible with God" (Mark 10:27). Faith sighed as a buzzer sounded.

"Well, finally—the limo is here." Boss grabbed his hat and coat. "Where's my scarf? I hung it right here by my winter coat. It's supposed to snow—oh, that means I probably won't make it in time for the Christmas play—you know, the weather, traffic and all. Tell Hope I'll make it next year."

Once in the limo, Boss pulled out his new success book. He certainly wanted to make the thirty-minute ride to the office worth something. The title of this one was *You Can Be Successful—Just Pay the Price.*

"Whatcha reading, Boss?" The driver, Gabriel, glanced in the mirror. "Surely not another book on success. I have told you the only book that will help you have real success is the Good Book."

Yeah, Gabe, Boss thought smugly, *you look like you've found success—driving a limo every day.* Boss flipped the window switch that separated him from the driver and buried his head in his success book.

Gabriel grabbed his Bible and lifted it to the privacy window. "Here's the book you need to read, Boss," he said over the speaker.

Great. Here he goes again. I like this limo driver the best, and I trust him with my kids, but he sure can be annoying. Boss lowered the window. "Gabe, I read the Bible when I was a child. I don't have time for it now—I'm too busy. I have a huge corporation to run, I have meetings with my stockbroker three times a week, I have to travel all over the world—I don't have time to read the Bible!"

Boss paused. He was getting riled. "Besides, I'm successful, so God is blessing me. That means my relationship with God is just fine. I must be doing something right if the Man Upstairs is blessing me financially."

"Having money doesn't mean you know God, Boss. In fact, having money can deceive us into thinking that we are living for God, but actually money is our idol. Jesus said that we cannot serve both God and money; we have to choose between the two and serve only one."

"But I give to charities. And I know Faith gives to the church."

"So then you're a tither?"

Boss laughed. "You've got to be kidding. That's Old Testament stuff. I give whatever my tax advisers tell me—whatever is needed to get me off the hook financially with the IRS. I do my part—I can assure you."

Gabriel prayed silently, then said, "Boss, if you give to God begrudgingly, you might as well keep your money. God wants a cheerful giver. You are prideful, Boss. You feel that you are successful because you have money. You build large buildings in your corporation, millions are spent on building your corporation, but you are building your kingdom, not God's Kingdom."

Gabriel came to a stop.

"What's going on, Gabe? I'm going to be late! Can't you go faster?"

"Sorry, Boss, the traffic is stopped. Looks like we'll be here a while." Gabriel watched as beautiful, fluffy snowflakes began to fall and realized he now had a captive audience.

"Boss," he said, as he opened his Bible, "I want to read something to you. Jesus talked about people who thought they knew God but really didn't. They thought they had done all the right things—giving money, working in the synagogues, doing the required religious acts of service—and they expected to go to heaven when they died because they did 'works.' Like you, they were building their own kingdoms, rather than focusing on building God's Kingdom."

Gabriel read:

> Then said one unto him, Lord, are there few that be saved? And he said unto them, Strive to enter in at the strait gate: for many, I say unto you, will seek to enter in, and shall not be able. When once the master of the house is risen up, and hath shut to the door, and ye begin to stand without, and to knock at the door, saying, Lord, Lord, open unto us; and he shall answer and say unto you, I know you not whence ye are: Then shall ye begin to say, We have eaten and drunk in thy presence, and thou hast taught in our streets. But he shall say, I tell you, I know you not whence ye are; depart from me, all ye workers of iniquity.
>
> Luke 13:23–27, KJV

"And Boss, I need to read just one more. Now listen; this one is really important."

> Children, how hard is it for them that trust in riches to enter into the kingdom of God! It is easier for a camel to

go through the eye of a needle, than for a rich man to enter into the kingdom of God.

Mark 10:24–25, KJV

Gabriel remained silent a few moments, allowing the words to penetrate his boss's heart, then asked, "Boss, do you understand that our works won't get us to heaven? We will get to heaven and not be allowed in. Jesus will say, 'Depart from me, you worker of iniquity.' See, we don't truly know Jesus as our Savior unless we build His Kingdom instead of ours."

Boss felt a tear forming in one eye. He reached for his handkerchief, but not in time to stop it from rolling down his cheek. God had pinpointed his iniquity. All these years he had not been convicted of his iniquity—but today he was checkmated by God.

Boss was softening. This traffic jam in the limo with Gabe had been a heavenly setup. "Gabe, I don't want to be turned away from God when I see Him. Iniquity. It sounds awful, and yet it's in my heart?"

I need it out, Boss thought. He looked up at the flurry-filled sky. *Forgive me, God. Teach me about the sin of iniquity so that I may truly know You.*

The traffic began to clear, and Gabriel pressed the gas pedal, maneuvering the limo into an intersection.

Bam! A large tour bus smashed into the side of the limousine. Gabriel was thrown sideways. Boss was thrown forward and into the side window.

Darkness. Blackness. Unconsciousness.

Ambulances took Gabriel and Boss to the nearest hospital. Gabriel began to recover during transport, and upon arrival at the hospital discovered that Boss was close to death. His thoughts were on Boss. *Lord, reach Boss. Don't*

70

let him die before he knows You. He watched as medical personnel rushed Boss past him on a gurney—unconscious, bleeding, barely breathing and headed for surgery.

The Experience

A bright light stirred Boss and seemed to awaken him from the darkness. Was he in heaven? Could he hope to be in heaven? Angels were spinning around him—confusion surrounded him.

Slowly things began to clear. He realized he was watching a group of angels quarreling.

"Lucifer, we have to talk!"

Lucifer had a position in heaven above many others. There were numerous other cherubs, but he was *the* cherub—the one entrusted with guarding God's throne. Boss watched Lucifer carefully and studied his actions.

Lucifer straightened to stand taller than the others. Like a proud peacock, he lifted his head above theirs. He was fascinated with the light that exuded from his own being—and yet he continually measured his light against God's.

I will ascend to heaven and establish my throne! These words were wedged deep within every chamber and crevice of Lucifer's heart. Jealousy, envy and pride provoked his every move. "I am an anointed cherub," he boasted. "God placed me above the rest. I am the most anointed of all, entrusted with so much more than the others. Therefore, I am also one chosen to lead. I am successful—I am guaranteed success. I am full of splendor."

Lucifer planted the seeds and waited for a response from his listeners. Lucifer, the "Light-bearer," had a cancer growing within his heart.

71

Boss continued to study Lucifer—he identified with his pride, arrogance and competitive nature. He understood Lucifer's motives. *Could this be iniquity? Is this what iniquity looks like?*

Lucifer was bent on building his own kingdom. He did not just want to be like God; he wanted to *be* God, the boss. The pride and iniquity in his heart began to dim the light that came from him, yet he continued to boast, seeking a following.

"I will ascend to heaven and establish my kingdom. Come, follow me! I know how to build a kingdom!"

"You're exactly right! You do know so much concerning the Kingdom. All of the inner workings of heaven are within your reach," said one angel as he left the anointed angelic fold and stood beside Lucifer. Several others followed. And the closer they leaned into Lucifer, the dimmer their lights became.

One by one angels sided with Lucifer. Pride became their master. They were becoming enslaved to Lucifer and his deceptive ambitions. Pride became their champion and they chose to commit idolatry.

"I intend to set myself up as supreme!" Lucifer boasted. With each boast, this angel, hand-fashioned by God, lost more light. In his desire for others to pay him homage, he lost more and more of his brilliance. Yet his words were so sly and seductive that even more sided with him. An as-yet-unknown stirring evolved. Evil, an alien concept, had been birthed in heaven.

Other angels, however, hastened to the throne of their Lord. Not understanding this new presence in their midst, they sought out their Prince of Peace.

"What does Lucifer mean? How can he sit upon the mount of the congregation?" one angel questioned another.

"He means he will 'appoint' himself as God."

"Surely not? Who would ever believe him? Who would listen to his lies and deceit? Why would anyone follow Lucifer over God? Why would anyone follow his iniquity?"

Iniquity—I knew it! Boss thought. And then . . .

"Boss. Boss. Wake up, Boss. Can you hear me?" Gabe stood beside him. "Faith and the kids are almost here. The snow has held up traffic, but they should be here soon."

Boss, still drugged from the surgery, grasped Gabe's hand. "Gabe, I saw the devil! I saw how he seduced even the angels to follow him. He had iniquity, pride and arrogance in his heart. Gabe, I don't want to be like Lucifer. Can you help me? Will you pray for me now? Will God save me? I've been so prideful. I've been so interested in success, money and building my own kingdom. Can God ever forgive me?"

"He already has, Boss." Gabriel then proceeded to lead him into his destiny with God. Truly God had sent Christian a guardian angel.

The Beginning of Iniquity

Iniquity began in the heart of Satan. The prophet Ezekiel wrote about how God fashioned Lucifer so perfectly, and yet iniquity was found in Lucifer's heart: "Thou wast perfect in thy ways from the day that thou wast created, till iniquity was found in thee" (Ezekiel 28:15, KJV).

Isaiah 14 offers insight into Satan's iniquity:

How art thou fallen from heaven, O Lucifer, son of the morning! how art thou cut down to the ground, which didst weaken the nations! For thou hast said in thine heart, I will ascend into heaven, I will exalt my throne

73

above the stars of God: I will sit also upon the mount of the congregation, in the sides of the north: I will ascend above the heights of the clouds; I will be like the most High. Yet thou shalt be brought down to hell, to the sides of the pit.

verses 12–15, KJV

This passage refers to Satan's (Lucifer's) heart thoughts and lists five choices that Satan "willed" to do:

1. *I will* ascend into heaven. (Lucifer was full of pride and wanted God's throne.)
2. *I will* exalt my throne above the stars of God. (He wanted a throne above God's—talk about pride and arrogance!)
3. *I will* sit upon the mount of the congregation. (Satan wanted his own congregation. In the same way that God has His Bride, the Church, Satan wanted his own group of followers. Unfortunately, he now has one: those demons who followed him and the human beings who choose to worship Satan. How we have been deceived!)
4. *I will* ascend above the heights of the clouds. (Satan exhibited pride, competition, exaltation of self and deception at its worst.)
5. *I will* be like the most High. (Satan wants to be "higher" than the Most High God who created him.)

These attitudes of the heart were iniquity, and they caused God to throw Lucifer out of heaven. Let's take a more in-depth look at iniquity so that we can begin to examine our own hearts.

Iniquity

The word *iniquity* is defined several different ways in Scripture. The iniquity passed down through generations due to idolatry refers to the *evil* and *perversion* attached to the sin. The word is derived, however, from a root word meaning "perverse and perverted, crooked, (to be) bowed down, troubled, wrong and wicked."[1] The *iniquity* found in Satan's heart is translated more pointedly as "(to) distort, perverted and unrighteous."[2] It is easy to conclude that there is absolutely *nothing* good in the devil. He is evil; he distorts the truth; he is crooked and a crook; he causes trouble; he is wicked and perverted; he is totally unrighteous in every way possible.

Iniquity began with the devil, and he was cast out of heaven. Then in the Garden of Eden, Satan seduced Adam and Eve, and they became afflicted with iniquity. We humans have been at war with iniquity ever since. And now if we "bow down" to an idol of any type, we are cursed again with iniquity. Take a look at this:

> Thou shalt not make unto thee a *graven image*, nor any likeness of any thing that is in heaven above, or that is in the earth beneath, or that is in the water under the earth. Thou shalt *not bow down* thyself unto them, nor serve them, for I Jehovah thy God am a jealous God, visiting the iniquity of the fathers upon the children, upon the third and upon the fourth generation of them that hate me, and showing lovingkindness unto thousands of them that love me and keep my commandments.
>
> Exodus 20:4–6, ASV, emphasis added

Iniquity, therefore, is linked with idolatry. When God gave Moses the Ten Commandments, He made this quite clear.

What does He say will happen if a man bows down to a graven image? A curse of iniquity will come upon the man and his descendants to the third and fourth generation. In other words, if idolatry is present, then the sin of iniquity is passed down through the generations.

God's instructions not to sin in this fashion seem clear, right? Why, then, did the nation of Israel have one problem after another concerning idolatry? The main reason is iniquity. The main reason is iniquity. Israel was led into captivity because of their iniquity (see Isaiah 46:2). And because of sin, the iniquitous patterns affected the future generations (see Exodus 20:5). In other words, because of the idolatrous sin of their fathers, the children inherited iniquity.

Even today we can see generational strongholds upon our generations. Perhaps you have noticed a family "pattern" or a "bent" toward a perversion or addiction—drugs, alcohol or codependency, for example. These are generational iniquities.

Do you see the connection? Satan was cast out of heaven because he desired the worship that was given to God; and yes, he still desires that exalted position today. When we give him that exalted position in our lives and believe what he says above God's words concerning us, then we are committing idolatry. We then inherit his sin of iniquity and pass it down to our descendants.

 In addition to passing iniquity down to our descendants, iniquity also causes us to be separated from God. Psalm 66:18 says, "If I regard wickedness in my heart, the Lord will not hear" (NASB). Did you get that? If we allow iniquity to remain in our hearts, the Lord will not hear us! If we know iniquity is there, and yet pretend it is not there or even encourage it, then we are opening doors to demonic attacks and bondage, and we are closing the door to the Lord.

Satan's Seat of Authority

Where Satan has been allowed influence—especially through idolatry—he has a throne, or a seated position of ungodly and illegitimate authority. My good friend and anointed author and minister Chuck Pierce exposes idolatry in his insightful book, *The Future War of the Church*:

> Corporate sin—for example, idolatry, bloodshed, immorality and covenant breaking—creates a break in God's purpose, or order, for a region [of the world]. Once this break begins to occur, Satan will take advantage to gain an upper hand and begin to establish his influence in that area. From that place of influence, Satan can build a throne upon which he is seated in that territory.[3]

In other words, through idolatry and other sins, Satan's darkness can influence an entire region or territory, and the effects are further idol worship, perversion, works of the flesh, humanism and demonic influence in the arts, governments and educational systems.

According to Revelation 2:12–17, Satan had an earthly throne in Pergamum (from here forward referred to as Pergamos). Because of this, Satan had established a stronghold in that territory.

Concerning the city of Pergamos, *Unger's Bible Dictionary* states the following:

> The city [Pergamos] was greatly addicted to idolatry, and its grove, which was one of the wonders of the place, was filled with statues and altars. It was a sort of union of a

pagan cathedral city, a university town, and a royal residence, embellished during a succession of years by kings who all had a passion for expenditure and ample means of gratifying it. It was according to pagan nations a sacred place, a city of temples, devoted to sensual worship.[4]

Even the Lord addressed the church in Pergamos and pointedly addressed the fact that Satan was enthroned there:

These are the words of him who has the sharp, double-edged sword. I know where you live—*where Satan has his throne.* Yet you remain true to my name. You did not renounce your faith in me, even in the days of Antipas, my faithful witness, who was put to death in your city— *where Satan lives.*

Revelation 2:12–13, emphasis added

So Pergamos was wicked—a place where Satan was able to establish his reign. It was a city of great wealth, yet its wealth was used to lavish the temples of idols. And when money is used in an ungodly way, you can bet Mammon is active.

Tyre

Another biblical place where Satan had a stronghold of idolatry and iniquity was the city of Tyre. The Tyrians began as a Phoenician people, who were seafarers. Hiram, the king of Tyre, therefore, decided to build himself a palace in the sea. The only way to do that was to construct a man-made island out of solid rock on which to build the palace, and so he did. Historians speculate that the project employed thousands of people and took years to complete. When it was built, the island of solid rock was named *Tyre*, or "rock." It became a center of the ancient world.

Being an island offered a large degree of security. The city of Tyre was so well fortified that it deemed itself impregnable. Its location and security allowed it to become a great seafaring, naval and financial power, and for centuries it was considered the "Wall Street" of its time. So wealthy was the city of Tyre that its resources furnished Solomon's Temple. Second Chronicles 2 documents Solomon's desire to build God the most beautiful temple in the world, and he used vast resources sent from the king of Tyre (see verses 1–11).

To ensure the city's prosperity, the Tyrians honored the false god Baal (the son of the fish-god Dagon) and the sea god Melqart (the son of Poseidon). Theologian Boyd Rice states:

> Baal worship was so central to sea peoples that his name was often attached to the names of their city states. For instance, Tyre, Sidon and Hazon were once called Baal-Tyre, Baal-Sidon, and Baal-Hazon. In addition, Asarte (also known as Ashteroth) was worshiped as "lady of the sea." . . . Her cult is thought to have been transposed onto the Mary cult of Southern France. Interestingly, history records seven or eight crucified messiahs, all born of virgin births, and each having a mother named Mary (or some derivation thereof).[5]

So Tyre was founded upon a basis of idolatry and an antichrist belief system, spawned through Lucifer's pride, arrogance and rebellion. Since the city was built upon idolatrous worship, it represents a stronghold of the enemy concerning wealth, ungodly riches and power. Its ungodly quest for wealth opened the door to Mammon and the perversions of a Babylonian system. Also attached to this "rock" are pride, arrogance, covetousness, jealousy and building selfish kingdoms. Truly Tyre was Satan's domain.

Satan's Seated Position in Tyre

The entire chapter of Ezekiel 27 confirms Tyre's dominion, wealth, resources and beauty. It begins with a description of Tyre's perfection as a gateway to the sea:

> And say unto Tyrus, O thou that art situate at the entry of the sea, which art a merchant of the people for many isles, Thus saith the Lord GOD; O Tyrus, thou hast said, I am of perfect beauty. Thy borders are in the midst of the seas, thy builders have perfected thy beauty.
>
> verses 3–4, KJV

This chapter clearly delineates the amazing type of worldly influence that Tyre possessed.

After this incredible description, Ezekiel 28 presents God's correction and rebuke to the city and to the king of Tyre. In verse 2, God says the ruler of Tyre has the pride of Satan: "In the pride of your heart you say, 'I am a god; I sit on the throne of a god in the heart of the seas.'" Do you remember when Satan said "in his heart" that he would ascend above God and establish his throne? Here we have almost the same words. The king of Tyre echoes the iniquity of Satan. Satan's haughty spirit also operated in the king of Tyre; his spiritual being was manifested in mankind.

The verse continues, "But you are a man and not a god, though you think you are as wise as a god." Clearly, in this passage God is addressing a mere man and not Satan. We certainly discern, however, Satan's influence and his seated position in Tyre.

God goes on to address the treasuries and wealth of Tyre. He says that "because of your wealth your heart has grown proud" (verse 5). Pride is often an offspring of wealth, but God was not addressing simply the king of Tyre's pride; he was addressing his idolatry. Money, wealth, fame and success had become the king's gods.

God goes on to tell the king that because the king thought himself as wise as a god, God would bring him down with foreign swords and he would die a violent death in the heart of the seas. Indeed, what this king built would eventually destroy him.

It is always this way with idol worship. The false god to which we bow down will take us to the pit, just as God declared over the king (see verses 1–10.)

Then God compares the iniquity of Lucifer to the iniquity of the king of Tyre. Observe the Word of the Lord in Ezekiel to the king of Tyre, a mere man:

> Moreover the word of the LORD came unto me, saying, Son of man, take up a lamentation upon the king of Tyrus, and say unto him, Thus saith the Lord GOD; Thou sealest up the sum, full of wisdom, and perfect in beauty.
>
> Ezekiel 28:11–12, KJV

Then in verse 13 God begins to address the characteristics of Satan that also are found in the king of Tyre. Go to your Bible and read Ezekiel 28:11–19. Here God is actually describing the "cherub," Satan, and how he was perfect before iniquity was found in him:

1. Satan was an anointed cherub who rebelled due to iniquity in his heart.
2. He was beautiful and therefore became prideful and fell.
3. He cultivated iniquity in the temples (seduced the priesthood into sin).
4. His "trafficking" (businesses and trade) were also influenced through iniquity.
5. He became a "terror" to all connected (agreeing) with him.

This chapter in Ezekiel describes how the cherub, Satan, walked on God's holy mountain and was blameless until iniquity was found in him. He was proud because of his perfection and beauty; he felt wiser than God. God therefore cast him out of heaven. Pride in one's beauty and perfectionism come from the evil spirit of Satan. And God declared him to be a "terror." Pride, arrogance, love of self, selfish ambition, perfectionism and building our own kingdoms over God's Kingdom open doors to the tyrant, Satan, thus giving him a seated position.

In this chapter, then, the king of Tyre is Satan personified. In other words, Satan's spiritual being was manifested in mankind. My co-laborer, author Cindy Jacobs, states in her awesome book *Exposing the Gates of the Enemy* that kings and rulers upon the earth have been influenced by Satan himself:

Understanding the passage in Isaiah 14 when Satan exalts himself by saying, "I will ascend; I will arise and sit upon the mount of the congregation," etc., opens doors to greater understanding of the king of Tyre: the ungodly king over trade, commerce and wealth. It is the same spirit of pride, greed and ungodly spirits of wealth that we battle today. Remember: Anytime we feel we can fend for ourselves without God's help we are committing idolatry.[6]

So the king of Tyre, the king over trade, commerce and wealth in the ancient world, was Satan personified. Again, this does not mean that trade, commerce and wealth are in and of themselves iniquitous. Rather, the king's ungodly idolatry of those things was blatant iniquity.

Wall Street

Satan himself, then, influenced the king of Tyre to build an abomination to the Lord. In the same way today, Satan influences the "kings" of the world to build abominations: centers of financial and economic power that serve as idols to many. There are 383 different financial centers of power in the world today, yet the most historic one is in lower Manhattan, New York City, New York. It is the first permanent home of the New York Stock Exchange and is known as a district of influential financial interests of the American financial industry. Named for the street on which it is located, it is called Wall Street.

Let me say again that making money is not a bad thing. Indeed, capitalism is not in and of itself an ungodly pursuit. Rather, it is the idolatry of Wall Street that has caused many in our nation—and throughout the world—to suffer from iniquity. It is the elevation of Wall Street above God, the elevation of money (Mammon) above the things of God, that is idolatrous. And it is the pride in Wall Street that leads people into such idolatry—the same pride that Satan had in his heart.

83

During the recent stock market crash our economy plummeted and the value of money fell. Those who had put their trust in money suffered greatly with depression, anxiety, even suicide. Their money was their security, and when it was gone, what was left?

Dear ones, our trust must be completely in the Lord—not money (Mammon). The king of Tyre was brought down because his trust was in Mammon. He built an idol, an abomination to the Lord, based upon his pride, greed and selfishness.

Let us not fall into the same trap of Satan! Let us right now begin to overthrow Satan's seated positions!

Overthrowing Satan's Seated Positions

The world system, then, attempts to be exalted above God's government and His perfect will for us on the earth. Iniquity has defiled our world system and the wealth involved. This is one reason money has become an idol: We have been seduced to trust money over God.

Dear ones, it is time to overthrow Satan's seated position in our world system and in our lives. We cannot tolerate the enemy's seductions any longer. It is our season to repent, and I believe most Christians are aware of the necessity of repentance during these uncertain times. If we remain in pride, iniquity, rebellion and idolatry, building kingdoms on foundations of greed, competition, envy and covetousness, then we will fall just as Lucifer did: "There are the workers of iniquity fallen: they are cast down, and shall not be able to rise" (Psalm 36:12, KJV).

In closing, let's look once more at Revelation 2:12–17 and study the iniquitous pattern connected to Pergamos, the false god of Mammon and its connection to Balaam. If you remember, Jesus commended those who remained true to His name especially when under demonic pressure from Satan, Mammon and idolatry. However, He also corrected them for holding to the teaching of Balaam:

> Nevertheless, I have a few things against you: You have people there who hold to the teaching of Balaam, who taught Balak to entice the Israelites to sin by eating food sacrificed to idols and by committing sexual immorality. Likewise you also have those who hold to the teaching of the Nicolaitans. Repent therefore! Otherwise, I will soon come to you and will fight against them with the sword of my mouth. He who has an ear, let him hear what the Spirit says to the churches. To him who overcomes, I will give some of the hidden manna. I will also give him a white stone with a new name written on it, known only to him who receives it.
>
> Revelation 2:14–17

In the Old Testament, the prophet Balaam (of donkey fame) was asked by Balak, the king of Moab, to curse Israel. Balak told the prophet that if he did so he would reward him monetarily. (Warning! Mammon!) Balaam knew he could not curse Israel (see Numbers 23:21), but the prophet's heart was bent toward the profit and, therefore, his lust for money overpowered his anointing. Mammon actively perverted his motives.

Money was not the issue; rather, Balaam's lust for money was the problem. In fact, Balaam's spirit was so perverted that he sought alternative ways for Israel to be cursed. Balaam was completely deceived. He decided not to curse Israel directly but presented the king with a strategy to seduce Israel into idolatry by eating foods sacrificed to idols and committing immorality. This in itself brought a curse upon Israel—without the prophet's *declaring* a curse. Balaam thought this sly strategy gave him an out, but God knew his heart and motives.

In the book of Revelation God addressed Balaam as a false prophet. He was a false prophet because he had been influenced by the false god Mammon. This prophet bowed his knee to the love of money. Though God did not speak of Mammon when he named Balaam as a false prophet, it is obvious that Balaam had bowed down to this idol.

God says that like Balaam, the city of Pergamos had given a seat to Satan through idolatry and iniquity. He rebukes them for their unrighteousness, perversion and sin. But when God rebukes a church, city or individual, He always gives opportunity to repent and turn from wickedness, and He empowers His people to defeat the enemy and his strongholds.

In Revelation 2 God gives us the keys to unlock doors of victory against the perversion of Pergamos and Satan's seat. The keys are to:

1) Repent (see verse 16). Repentance always opens the door to freedom and victory. Remaining free and victorious, however, depends upon our choices after we repent. True repentance brings change.
2) Pray using God's "sharp, double-edged sword" (verse 12). This sword, we know, is God's Word, and we are to pray the Word over our lives, finances and even temptations so that we can defeat the enemy. Speaking the words God says about us will topple the throne of Satan when he attempts to remain in a seated position over us. Through this form of spiri-

tual warfare we can bind the enemy and gain God's victory.

God says that to those who overcome He will give the "hidden manna" (hidden revelation) and "a white stone with a new name written on it" (verse 17). While the enemy has named us "fearful," "rebellious," "stupid," "unwanted," "abandoned," "poor," "weak," "shameful," "wicked," "lovers of money," "unlawful," "unfaithful," "worthless," "idol worshipers," etc., God says that after our repentance He will rename us as "strong warriors with great faith," "the Bride of Christ," "beautiful," "obedient," "victorious," "loved," "accepted," "powerful," "unashamed," "rich in Christ," "lovers of God" and "forgiven."

I know you are an overcomer! So let's start right now with repentance. Grab that pen and journal once more for your next assignment. This will be a simple time of repentance, and I encourage you to take some time and allow the Holy Spirit to speak to your heart.

(For a more in-depth study and prayers to target specific strongholds, I recommend Neil T. Anderson and Rich Miller's book, *Walking in Freedom*.[7])

Assignment

1. As you have read this chapter, have you recognized iniquitous patterns in you or your generations? If so, write them below or in your journal.

Repent to God for each sinful pattern and receive His forgiveness.

2. Pride is a temptation for most of us, along with self-exaltation, selfishness and arrogance. Many times pride manifests in believing that our own wisdom is better than God's. In other words, we believe we know better than God—thus, we attempt to control our lives. Is this a problem for you also? If so, write areas in which you struggle below or in your journal.

_____

_____

_____

Repent for each area the Holy Spirit reveals, and then receive His forgiveness.

3. Have you been more interested in building your own kingdom rather than God's? Examine your life. Have you attempted to build up your ministry or career and become jealous over the successful ministries or careers of others? This is one indication of building personal kingdoms. Ask the Holy Spirit to show you if this is an iniquitous pattern in your life and then write it down.

_____

_____

_____

Repent to God for every area where you have pursued your own selfish interests rather than your godly assignments. Then repent for building your own kingdom. Receive His forgiveness.

4. Do you love money more than you desire to be obedient to God? If so, then you are being seduced by Mammon, and it is blocking your freedom. You cannot be free from iniquitous patterns without repentance. Write down areas in which the love of money has control of you.

_____

_____

_____

Repent for the love of money. Ask God how to change your false beliefs concerning money or any lack of it. Repent again if needed and receive His forgiveness.

5. Write down the names that Satan has called you. Then mark out each name and beside it write the true name that God has given you, which is opposite of what Satan has said. For example, instead of "rebellious," write "obedient."

_____

_____

_____

Renounce every name that the enemy has given you, even through other people. Ask God to forgive you for believing the lies of Satan. Then speak boldly your new name—the true name that God has given you. Receive His forgiveness and your new name!

Now pray with me:

Father, forgive us for all iniquity. We repent from our sin. Do not allow us to stumble and fall. You said that all of us have gone astray and have iniquity—yet Jesus took it to the cross. Thank You, Lord, for Your forgiveness. Thank You, Jesus, for nailing my iniquity to the cross. Thank You for giving me a new name! In Jesus' name, Amen.

Stand up and give the Lord a shout of praise. I am proud of how you have been so courageous and determined to shift into life and victory. You have spoken His Word and overcome the enemy. You are now an overcomer!

4

Understanding the Deceitfulness of Riches

And the one on whom seed was sown among the thorns, this is the man who hears the word, and the worry of the world and the deceitfulness of wealth choke the word, and it becomes unfruitful.

Matthew 13:22, NASB

J esus! Come quickly into the boat!" One of the disciples hastened Jesus to safety.

Multitudes thronged Jesus and His disciples, anxious to hear more about the Kingdom. Many had traveled vast distances to hear the Teacher. As they inched closer toward Him, the disciples realized the need for Jesus to step into a nearby boat for security.

Jesus' desire to sow the seeds of His Kingdom message always outweighed matters that seemed to press against Him. Although threats from mobs, religious systems and large crowding multitudes challenged the disciples, Jesus always remained at peace, knowing the Father had sent Him to teach the Good News of the Kingdom. Pointedly and without fear, Jesus positioned Himself inside the humble, primitive vessel—the Living Water upon the water—while continuing to teach the crowd concerning the Kingdom.

A perfect setting, Jesus thought. *A gentle breeze, the smell of the sea and a captive audience! Indeed, this is good soil into which I can sow the truth. Father, empower Me to speak about Your Kingdom today.* Jesus spoke with a love and godly authority that the crowds had never before witnessed. His tender smile answered the curiosity of the crowds, who came wondering if He was just another religious leader. His compassionate, loving eyes stilled hearts, and all skepticism banished as He spoke. Living Water gushed forth to quench and fill the empty, parched vessels.

He gave the same message as His forerunner, John the Baptist, who had taught, "Repent, for the Kingdom of Heaven is near." Yet Jesus expanded so much more on the Kingdom. The earthly kingdom in which the citizens lived was militant, cruel and taxing. Their "king" was Caesar, the Roman emperor. Yet the Teacher spoke of a Kingdom of love, peace and joy. He traveled throughout Galilee teaching in synagogues, preaching the Good News of the Kingdom and healing all kinds of diseases and sicknesses—leprosy, severe pain, demon possession, paralysis, seizures, blindness. No matter what the challenge, Jesus taught, healed and ministered life.

The Gospel He taught was simple, yet the hidden mysteries within His incredible stories intrigued every listener. Teaching in parables confounded their minds, yet their hearts were pierced and they were compelled to follow Him. His teachings challenged the religious system, confronted the Pharisees and exposed sin. The Kingdom to which He referred was paradoxical—one had to die to live in it, to be last in order to be first in it and to be lost in order to be found. The Teacher stressed that many would hear but not understand His message.

Jesus continued to teach from the boat, this time in the form of a parable:

> A farmer went out to sow his seed. As he was scattering the seed, some fell along the path, and the birds came and ate it up. Some fell on rocky places, where it did not have much soil. It sprang up quickly, because the soil was shallow. But when the sun came up, the plants were scorched, and they withered because they had no root. Other seed fell among thorns, which grew up and choked the plants. Still other seed fell on good soil, where it produced a crop—a hundred, sixty or thirty times what was sown. He who has ears, let him hear.
>
> Matthew 13:3–9

"Is this the message concerning the Kingdom?" many in the crowd asked. They heard Him, but they did not fully understand His teaching. "How does one sow properly, and how does a person sow and yield a crop a hundred times more than what has been sown? What could this mean?"

Understanding Is for Disciples

The disciples approached Jesus. They recognized a truth being told, yet no one understood it. "Why do You talk to people in parables? What is the meaning of these stories? We do not understand!"

Jesus patiently explained to His disciples that the mysteries of the Kingdom were not for others to understand. Rather, the hidden meanings of His parables were for those to whom He referred as His disciples. A *disciple* is more than a mere pupil; a *disciple* is a follower. The term relates to one who not only *hears* but also seeks to *understand*. It refers to the student who is not simply open to gaining more knowledge but who also is committed to understanding what is taught, who is not just receiving "head knowledge" but is pairing that head knowledge with spiritual understanding.

Many of Jesus' listeners heard Him but had calloused hearts. They gained head knowledge but closed their eyes to spiritual understanding (see Matthew 13:16–17). Yet His disciples submitted to the teachings of Jesus to gain understanding. Standing against their natural reasoning, they allowed the Spirit of God to lead them and chose to follow Him and submit to His teachings. Because they proved themselves in this way, the Lord related to them the meanings of His parables and unfolded for them the mysteries concerning the Kingdom of God.

We, too, are called to be Jesus' disciples. In church we are taught head knowledge concerning Kingdom revelation, but we have to study Scripture, delving deeper into God's Word, in order to gain spiritual knowledge. Only then can God breathe His *rhema*—life-giving revelation—on us, and only then can His Holy Spirit inspire our understanding.

Only then can we experience the "Spirit of wisdom and of understanding" (Isaiah 11:2), which overshadows us and manifests to us as one of the seven-fold manifestations of the Spirit of God. Indeed, Jesus calls we who are His disciples blessed because He desires to share the mysteries of the Kingdom with us.

A Spiritual Look at the Parable of the Sower

I know you desire to dig deeper and gain that spiritual knowledge, or you would not have decided to read this book. So, disciples of God, let's take a look at the mystery concerning the parable of the sower. Because it involves the deceitfulness of riches, we must dig deeply into revelation concerning the soil of our hearts. Grab your Bible (a New International Version is preferable) and read the parable of the sower in Matthew 13:18–23.

Now let's look at what Jesus said.

1. *We must understand the message of the Kingdom.*
Jesus talked about the person who hears the message and does not understand it. He said that the enemy comes and snatches the message away from such a person's heart. The word *understand* in this passage means not only to put facts together and consider something, but also to use wisdom. When a person hears the message from the Father, therefore, he must use wisdom to gain understanding and then act upon it in faith. If the person only hears and never understands because the soil of his heart is hard, then the thief will attempt to steal, kill and destroy. Hearing but not understanding opens doors to the enemy, who steals the Word from one's heart. Many times, however, simply stepping out on God's commands by faith will allow later

understanding to follow. But if one's heart is hard, then it is difficult to step out in faith at all—all the more reason to allow the Lord to soften his or her heart.

This explains why Jesus did not fully reveal the parable; He desired disciples who truly hungered to understand what He was teaching. Why sow seed if people were not truly hungry to receive it? It would be a waste of time. And Jesus was dangling a carrot before the people, making them hungrier to understand.

It is a simple message, really: Receive the truth in your heart, ask the Holy Spirit to bring full understanding and then use wisdom to act upon what you know. Faith without works is dead—but works without faith also are dead. If we believe and receive Truth, then we will act upon the revelation. And if we are workers in the Kingdom of Heaven, then we must apply faith to what we do for the King of the Kingdom. Acting upon God's Word requires faith.

When we hear the Word and do not act, then we allow a death structure to be built. As I described in chapter 2, a death structure occurs when the enemy is able to steal truth, replace it with a lie and build a structure or fortress (stronghold) around it. Therefore, when we hear the Word, we must use wisdom and act upon it, or else the enemy will come and snatch the Word from our hearts.

Gaining wisdom, then, is the key. First Kings 4:29–30 tells us:

> God gave Solomon wisdom and understanding exceeding much, and largeness of heart, even as the sand that is on the sea-shore. And Solomon's wisdom excelled the wisdom of all the children of the east, and all the wisdom of Egypt.
>
> ASV

Note that Solomon never asked for riches, wealth, honor or even a long life; instead he asked for wisdom and knowledge, so that as king he could rightly judge God's people (see 2 Chronicles 1:10–12). Yet because his heart was right, God gave him his request and blessed him with wisdom beyond any other man who has ever lived, as well as with great riches and wealth. If Solomon had asked for riches rather than wisdom, God stated that He would not have blessed him to the degree that He did.

Dear believers, this is a revelation that we all need! God wants us to be like Solomon. If we ask God for wisdom above all else, then He also is able to bless us with wealth and riches. In other words, if we desire God's wisdom, which is linked with understanding, then prosperity follows. It is a heart attitude, plain and simple.

The Body of Christ needs a spiritual heart bypass. We have to bypass what we think in the natural and learn to respond from our hearts. What we think is wisdom—such as asking God for more money—is not His wisdom. Rather, God's wisdom is seeking Him first—and *then* all things are added unto us. "Seek ye first the kingdom of God, and his righteousness; and all these things shall be added unto you" (Matthew 6:33, KJV). Rather than spending hours laboring over prayers for wealth, why not simply seek Him first, and then He can add "all things"?

2. *The seeds taught must take root (see Matthew 13:20–21).*

Jesus first encouraged His disciples to hear and understand, and to receive the Word with great joy. If the seed (the Word) fell upon rocky soil, however, then it could not take deep root. In rocky soil the seed (or the truth of God's Word) can be sustained only for a short time. When trouble or persecution comes because of the Word—and it will come!—then the one who receives the seed into stony places will quickly fall away.

To fall away in this passage is the Greek word *skandadlizo* (the root of our English word *scandalize*) and means "to entrap, trip up, stumble, to entice to sin, commit apostasy." It also means "to offend or be offended due to an offense."[1]

Are you easily offended? If so, then perhaps you are receiving the Word into rocky soil.

Think of how many times, for example, we ask God to make us wealthy, rich and prosperous and then become offended when God does not bring those things to pass in our lives. Because His Word is shallow in our hearts and we seek wealth and worldly gain over relationship, He postpones certain breakthroughs for our own good. He loves us too much to grant everything we pray. Often our response is to be angry with God rather than seek Him more. We may even reject (punish) Him when we do not receive what we desire. Dear believers, this is the purest test of true relationship with God. Responding properly proves our heartfelt relationship with Him. If we serve Him only because our every prayer is answered, then we do not have a pure relationship with Him. He is not Santa Claus; He is God and He knows what we need even before we ask.

I am not advocating that we should not ask the Lord for our needs and desires. I am saying, however, that we must be willing to wait patiently for His perfect will to be made manifest.

Jesus said that if our hearts have good soil, then we will not be easily offended. The good soil refers to a heart that is soft and not hardened. Trusting God for provision is a faith test and a chance to examine the hardness of our hearts. Let's not allow a test of our faith to become a weapon for the enemy to scandalize us and tempt us to commit apostasy and sin.

3. *The seeds must be sown into soil that is free of thorn-covered weeds, or else the thorns (deceitfulness of riches) will choke the infant seedlings as they begin to grow (see Matthew 13:22).*

Jesus said that seed could be sown and a man could "hear and even understand" the Word, but if the soil was full of thorn-covered weeds, then little fruit could grow there. Thorns are symbolic of a cursed ground that cannot be fruitful. Jeremiah warned Israel to "break up your fallow ground, and do not sow among thorns" (Jeremiah 4:3, NASB).

Jesus taught that the thorns were the worries of life and the "deceitfulness of wealth," which choke out the Word. Pay attention, now: Here we see Mammon exposed!

The "deceitfulness of riches" along with the "worries of life" will "choke" out the seed (the Word). Jesus gives us three things on which to focus here: 1) the deceitfulness of riches, 2) the worries of life and 3) choking. They all are related to each other.

Many worries of life are caused by our concern about provision. Of course, we are concerned about other issues, such as health, family, business, etc., but worry over finances is often the number one concern for people. If we do not trust God for our provision, then the enemy chokes the Word out of us—causing us no longer to believe our loving Father's desire to provide for us. Each time we fight doubt and unbelief concerning provision, Mammon is involved.

The word *choke* means "to strangle completely" (like death) and "to drown or to throng (crowd)."[2] Precious ones, Satan desires to crowd us with lies concerning provision. We must be on guard and realize that riches can be deceitful. If we love riches, then we can become deceived, and life is therefore choked out of us.

Jesus actually uses the term *deceitfulness of riches*. How do riches deceive us? Let's examine the word *deceitful* in this passage so that we do not simply hear but understand.

Strong's ties *deceitfulness* to "delusion."[3] Deception is a foundational stone upon which Satan builds his death structures. If he can seduce us with his lies, then he can deceive, or delude, us. Once we are deceived, he moves in with a truckload of more lies. His list of lies goes on and on. At times he attempts to be bigger than God—especially when it comes to provision. When we believe his lies, then we find ourselves strapped into an emotional roller coaster! We waver in our faith and are tossed to and fro.

How can we recognize a lie concerning Mammon (money, provision and the deceitfulness of riches)?

Consider just a few examples:

"God is not big enough to supply my need."

"God provides for others but not for me."

"I am such a mess that God will not care for me."

"God will not open doors for me concerning a job."

"I do not trust God to lead me to the right place of employment."

"I do not need to tithe; the church has enough money already."

"God does not need my money. How will it benefit Him anyway?"

"I like to control my money. Why ask God to get involved with my finances?"

"I do not go to church because all they want is my money."

"God wants to withhold from me. He does not trust or love me enough to bless me."

When we learn to recognize lies like these, then we can more easily and quickly see Satan's deception and the influence of Mammon in our lives. Jeremiah encouraged God's children to become circumcised unto Him and not unto the world. If His children refused, God's wrath would go forth like fire because of their evil hearts. God's standard for our hearts does not allow thorns, thistles, hardheartedness, stubbornness, doubt, unbelief, offenses or the love of money.

Eve was beguiled, or *deceived,* in the Garden. Satan tempted her to believe his lies concerning her future: "I am being left out" and "God does not desire to bless me." He challenged her identity and self-worth. She trusted the voice of the devil over what God had promised. Satan, capitalizing on her receiving his deception, choked the life out of her, and therefore a curse—or death structure—came upon entire generations. Thorns and thistles were part of that curse. The ground into which their seed was to be sown would be cursed with thorns and therefore not fully able to receive fruitfulness (see Genesis 3:18).

Satan challenges our identities and self-worth in the same ways today. When we compare ourselves with the "Joneses" next door, we often have an identity crisis. We do not have as large a house, or as elaborate furnishings or as much money. Our self-worth is often woven together tightly with riches, and when we feel less than someone else, the comparison makes us tempted to have "things."

Satan tells us we are not favored unless we experience material gain, and we choke on his lies.

This is an improper understanding of godly prosperity; it certainly is not the pure Gospel of the Kingdom! Yes, we are to believe for abundance, but along the way we must realize that we as individuals are valuable—whether we have money or not. Believers, our value is not based on things. Our value was established at the cross.

And before Jesus was raised up on that cross, man placed a crown of thorns on His head. I believe this crown symbolizes Christ taking the curse to the cross for us. What His enemies meant for harm and shame Jesus used for our redemption. Hallelujah! In the power of His resurrection, He exchanged a crown of curses for the crown of life. If we trust in Him and not riches, then we can receive life and the crown of life.

> Blessed is the man who perseveres under trial, because when he has stood the test, he will receive the crown of life that God has promised to those who love him.
>
> James 1:12, NIV

Dear reader, hear me: The love of wealth and the deceitfulness of riches can easily deceive us if our hearts are seeded with thorns. In fact, according to Jeremiah 12:13, Israel sowed wheat, but reaped thorns because of her sin. Precious saints, the Church is being called to an altar of repentance because of our materialism and love of money. True riches involve sacrifice unto God, laying down our lives and serving Him and not money.

4. *Seed needs good soil in which to produce a crop (see Matthew 13:23).*

Good soil involves hearing and understanding. Yet it is more than that. Good soil *produces*. Good soil yields a crop of "a hundred, sixty or thirty times what was sown" (Matthew 13:23). This passage does not say that any other soil produces—only the good soil produces.

One of the translations for *good soil* uses the word *virtue*, or *dunamis*, which is the miraculous power of God.[4] This is where we get our English word *dynamite*.

The word *dunamis* is used in the New Testament story of the woman with the issue of blood. When she pressed through the crowd, she in great faith touched the hem of Jesus' garment and was immediately healed. Jesus said that He felt "virtue" leave His body as she touched Him (see Luke 8:46, KJV). This poor, sick woman was "good soil," believing in faith as she pressed through the crowd. When she touched Jesus, virtue flowed forth, and she received her miracle.

Wow! The power of one sick woman's faith! Imagine the torment she had suffered for years, yet she chose not to be offended with God. Instead her heart chose to press beyond all doubt, unbelief, failure, oppression and rejection. The soil of her heart was good. Her heart was cleansed and she received her miracle.

Furthermore, Luke 6:19 says, "And the whole multitude sought to touch him: for there went *virtue* out of him, and healed them all" (KJV, emphasis added). A spiritual explosion of power—like dynamite—took place as Jesus became ignited to fulfill the Father's will upon the earth. Virtue, then, is exponential!

When our hearts are virtuous, we can touch God with sincere prayers and He will pour out a blessing that we will not be able to contain. A virtuous heart will *press* for the breakthrough but not *pressure* God with endless prayers for riches. A virtuous heart trusts for God's best, seeking Him first and trusting Him to pour out His blessing in His timing.

Are You Ready for Your Harvest?

The deceitfulness of riches can block the harvest. A *harvest* is a form of reaping, but *harvest* also implies "fruitfulness."[5]

In Genesis 1:28, God blessed Adam and Eve and told them to be fruitful and multiply. Fruitfulness, then, is part of God's blessing. So what does "being fruitful" involve? I believe that for far too long we have equated fruitfulness with financial wealth.

Biblical fruitfulness involves multiplication, growth and increase—and yes, the bearing of fruit. Bearing fruit is more that a peach tree producing more peaches year after year. Of course, when the peach farmer reaps a greater peach crop each season, he experiences increase and prosperity. And, yes, God wants us to prosper. But if the peach farmer trusts in peaches for provision rather than God, then he has a problem, for he is not trusting Jehovah Jireh, his Provider.

We, as disciples, should be increasing in our faith, becoming more Christlike, and transforming into His image. Good soil brings forth good fruit. If we are growing the fruit of the Spirit, then our hearts are good soil and we will receive the blessing of fruitfulness.

If, on the other hand, the soil of our hearts is evil, then our fruit is evil—and we therefore need the fire of God to purge us. Matthew 3:10 speaks of the axe being laid at the root of every tree that does not bring forth good fruit. These trees are cut down and cast into the fire.

John the Baptist stated that he, as a man, could baptize people in water, as a symbol of their repentance. But each still had to be baptized in the Holy Spirit and in fire (see Matthew 3:11). Dear ones, the fire must come. It is unavoidable for us who believe. To state that we must never suffer is to say that God has not baptized us with His Spirit. The fire is meant to purify us and not to harm us. John 15:2 says branches that bear no fruit are cut away and even cleansed. Believers, unless there is cleansing and fire, there is no blessed fruit—according to God's standards. Our bank accounts can be overflowing with money, but we are blessed only if God states we are blessed. And blessings and fruitfulness require the fruit of repentance.

We should be developing "fruit worthy of repentance" (Matthew 3:8, ASV) and "fruit that will last" (John 15:16). Fruit worthy of repentance is the message of the Kingdom that John the Baptist preached: "Bring forth therefore fruits meet for repentance" (Matthew 3:8 KJV). Repentance is an absolute necessity for healing, deliverance from strongholds and yielding fruit. In fact, it is clear that we cannot be in God's Kingdom unless we have the heart of repentance—a heart that is not hardened but rather is marked by the softness of good soil. And the fruits of repentance must be evident; that is, a person's repentance proves itself when the person who repented exhibits true turning and change. If we therefore do not see change in our own lives, then we need to examine the soil of our hearts and be sure it is "good soil" because we have truly repented for our sins.

One final point regarding repentance: We must be reminded that sin blocks breakthroughs and increase. One of my recent books, *Breaking the Threefold Demonic Cord*, exposes the strategies of the Jezebel spirit, which blocks repentance. For further information on this subject, I encourage you to read that book.

For too long we have focused on the fruitfulness of sowing money to reap money. God says that if we seek the Kingdom above all else, then all things will be added to us. This is the harvest. If we develop the fruit of the Spirit in hearts that are the soft, ready ground of good soil, then all things, including miracles and financial breakthroughs, will follow.

Jesus said:

> Ye have not chosen me, but I have chosen you, and ordained you, that ye should go and bring forth fruit, and that your fruit should remain: that whatsoever ye shall ask of the Father in my name, he may give it you.
>
> John 15:16, KJV

As "chosen" ones, we need to bring forth fruit that remains, fruit that abides by the Vine, and only then can we ask of the Father so that He gives us blessings. Our fruit that remains—or work that lasts—upon the earth is that which is done solely because the Father has ordained it. Otherwise, our works are burned in the fires of wood, hay and stubble. How can we ask the Father only for money and blessings when our hearts are not purified? Yet if we seek first His Kingdom, then He will bless us. How simple can that be, dear ones? First the fire, then the repentance, then the fruit—and therefore, the blessing.

Being blessed means being spiritually prosperous. Only those who understand true riches will be blessed. Only those who understand their need for God will prosper. True Kingdom prosperity does not come from money, but from being obedient to God. I do not want to be deceived by riches. I want to reap God's true harvest. Don't you?

106

In closing, let's take a quick peek at Galatians 5:22–26:

But the fruit of the Spirit is love, joy, peace, longsuffering, kindness, goodness, faithfulness, meekness, self-control; against such there is no law. And they that are of Christ Jesus have crucified the flesh with the passions and the lusts thereof. If we live by the Spirit, by the Spirit let us also walk. Let us not become vainglorious, provoking one another, envying one another.

ASV

When I read this passage, I always see something for which I need to repent. I want to reap a harvest, yet I see things in my heart that I do not admire. Do you?

Would you join me for a time of repentance?

Father, I know that my heart is not completely good soil. I want to be fruitful and multiply, but I want it to be so I can glorify You. I repent of selfishness, coveting, competitiveness and envy. I repent that I am not long-suffering, patient, good and kind. I repent for my lack of self-control and the lusts of the flesh. I also repent of (list here some areas of which the Holy Spirit has spoken to you while reading this chapter).

Father, I want good fruit to remain. I realize that good fruit comes only by abiding in You. I choose to remain connected to the Vine. I declare that I will not focus on money, but I will seek first the Kingdom of God. In Jesus' name, Amen.

5

Our Treasure Is Where
Our Hearts Are

Lay not up for yourselves treasures upon the earth, where moth and rust consume, and where thieves break through and steal: but lay up for yourselves treasures in heaven, where neither moth nor rust doth consume, and where thieves do not break through nor steal: for where thy treasure is, there will thy heart be also.

Matthew 6:19–21, ASV

While I have been writing this book, the enemy has challenged me with the spirits of Mammon and Babylon. We discussed in chapter 1 how Mammon opens the door to a spirit of bondage and slavery, and I am guilty of falling into these snares of the enemy. Indeed, as I have been writing to expose the spirit of Mammon, I have been warring against and overcoming the same spirit. So you see, I have personally experienced the deception of Mammon and Babylon, and through this experience my passion for helping you battle against these strongholds has been kindled afresh. I would like to share with you my struggle, in the hope that it will help you in yours.

My struggle is in no way connected to writing this book for money. I can assure you that one who has a heart bent for God's purposes would not be empowered to write on the evil seductions of Mammon and Babylon out of greed. Yet on this day, May 24, 2009, I admit to having had a serious heart check concerning greed, dissatisfaction, fear of loss, lack of trusting God and worry. Indeed, I confess to you that during the writing of this book the Lord has had to correct my grumbling and complaining.

You see, I was a city gal—totally city. I have always said that I was born for such a time as this, when our Western world boasts indoor restrooms rather than outhouses, air conditioning, concrete streets and sleek automobiles.

Yet I decided I wanted a horse. Well, acquiring a horse would require a barn, which would require land, which would require a move to the country—do you see where this story is headed?

Where did this desire come from? Was I crazy? Was it a mid-life crisis? I think maybe yes and yes.

I had owned several horses as a teenager, but I never had any really good experiences with any of them. I would get bucked off and end up with painful bruises and even broken arms. One day, for example, I was home alone and decided to barrel race in the pasture. I had already been kicked during a rodeo ride a few weeks earlier, when the nails of a horseshoe had dug deep into my leg, causing blood poisoning. So already injured, I decided to ride alone that day. As I did, my horse slipped on a water hose and fell on her side, trapping me between her and the dirt. She and I lay unconscious for several hours until my dad found us. Off to the hospital we rushed amidst my many tears. I will never forget the pain in my leg or the concern on my dad's face. I injured the same leg that had been hurt a few weeks before and almost lost the entire leg. But thanks to God and His healing power, my injuries eventually healed—although it took months and even today that leg is vulnerable to injury. So with this as my background, I felt I must have been crazy to want horses again.

Yet while my sister and I cared for my mother during her terminal, six-month battle with liver cancer, I developed an interest in horses again. You see, my mother's personal nurse raised thoroughbreds. When she told me of her ranch I immediately bombarded her with questions such as, "How many horses do you have?" "Do you ride?" "What are your horses' names?" "How long have you lived on your ranch?" I think I asked more about her animals than I did about her. Every time she came to check on Mom, I drilled her about her horses. Within one week of meeting her, I was inviting myself to her ranch to see the horses. During Mom's battle with cancer, Mom's nurse and I became friends, and I found myself spending entire days at her ranch. I believe that doing so offered me some glimpse of life in the middle of so much pain and heart-ache. I realize that my initial interest in horses was a godly distraction and an escape from the emotional pain concerning my mother's failing health. But my lasting passion for horses definitely was renewed, and I have questioned myself time and time again as to the reason why.

Before Mom went to heaven, I had bought my own horse. Now I have eight and still more babies coming! Indeed, the desire to have horses again led to our move to a 54-acre ranch and all that comes with it—a barn, fencing, wolves, snakes and other varmints. Talk about culture shock! This city girl honestly thought she could handle this move, but it turns out I have been challenged in every way possible.

As we transitioned to the country, my emotions ran amuck. I questioned my decisions and myself. Negative thoughts filled my mind with doubt, fear and anxiety. I began to suffer physically as I questioned God over and over if I had missed hearing Him and His direction. I drilled Mickey over and over (and over!) again: "Mick, do you really believe God is in this move? I feel so drawn to the country, but it goes against all reason."

It was true. Our move did not make sense. First, we did not have time for horses and a ranch. Second, I was worried about the money. Moving to the country was expensive in every way, and we certainly did not take up a huge offering at a speaking engagement one weekend so that we could buy a ranch! No, indeed. As custom homebuilders for years before we became ordained ministers, Mickey and I had been blessed financially. And being frugal, we had wisely invested our money and served as good stewards of what God gave us. Doing so eventually empowered us to travel more for the Lord and to do the work He called us to do. But now we were spending money for a lifestyle centered on a passion for horses, and I was holding tight to the purse strings. I lost sleep as I worried about our investments and fretted over our future. Would we continue to have enough money to feed the horses? What if we decided we were not happy in the country and had to sell for less? What if we totally ran out of money and ended up on the streets? What if . . . what if . . . what if? I was challenged every day with emotions I had not experienced in years.

"Sandie," Mickey reassured me, "God wants to give you the desires of your heart. He will supply the finances and care for us. Remember what His Word says: If we delight ourselves in the Lord, He will give us the desires of our hearts" (see Psalm 37:4).

His statement took my breath away. I had heard that Scripture preached many times, so why was it so hard for me to accept? I knew God wanted to bless me; that was not my issue. It was having the desires of my heart that challenged my faith.

What Was My Treasure?

I was struggling with a deep-rooted spiritual issue. I knew that setting my heart toward things—"treasure"—rather than on God's Kingdom was fruitless. I knew that I should be setting my heart on doing the will of God and seeking first His Kingdom. And then all these things—horses, land, blessings, breakthroughs, etc.—would be added to Mickey and me. Yet I struggled with the question: Were these desires of my heart—the horses—just "treasure"?

If we set our hearts toward things rather than His Kingdom, then those things become our treasure. If we set our hearts toward selfish gain, then we will open doors for chronic dissatisfaction. It is only when we set our hearts toward the Kingdom that we are truly blessed and fully satisfied. True treasure is knowing God and doing His perfect will. I knew all this and yet worried. . . .

In addition to struggling with the spiritual issues, this move pushed me further into a heated battle against Mammon. Financially, we felt it better to move into the small ranch house on the land rather than custom build a new one. The house was small, and we therefore had to downsize from our previous large home. Downsizing sounds like a good idea—until you realize that you are really and truly sizing *down*. That means a lot of things have to be tossed or given away. I could not fit all our furniture in our new home. Items that were both costly and precious to me were hauled to Goodwill, but I did not "will" to give them. I wanted to keep everything, yet could not. Rather than focusing on being used by God to bless someone else with this "stuff," I murmured and complained—a lot! I was toe-to-toe with Mammon.

Then within a week of moving, we decided to remodel. What a mess! This "dream" move to the country began to feel more like insanity than a blessing, and it turned out to be one of the biggest ordeals of my life.

And the situation snowballed even further. One month after our financial plunge and move to the country, the economy crashed. While today I realize that a failing economy does not negate God's promises, I must confess to you that at the time Mammon and the fear of losing what we had invested challenged my faith. I battled Mammon and fear of failure, and I worried about our decision. Was it right? My faith had taken a downward spiral.

Everything seemed to be going wrong for us. I doubted our every move. I tried to remember that we believed God had led us to the ranch. Deep down inside I really knew we had been obedient by moving to the country and that God wanted to give me the desires of my heart. And yet . . . the barn was not finished, we were behind on the fencing, and the subcontractors were delayed. To top it all off I had

114

little—and I do mean *little*—closet space for my clothes. This truly was a national disaster in the Freed household.

I need closets! I murmured daily. *I need shelves! I need a drawer for my makeup! I need space for my blow-dryer! I, I, I, me, me, me!* My inner struggle was not so inner anymore.

Mickey would grow silent, take a deep breath and head out to the barn. *Why in the world is he going to the barn when I need my closet fixed?* I would wonder. Never mind that we had pregnant horses about to deliver.

This was my dream come true—so why was I fussing so much? I seemed to focus only on the fact that it had cost more money than we had planned, my time was being stolen, my husband "was not there for *me*," the economy was spiraling down, etc. What was wrong with me?

It was Mammon, pure and simple. My heart had been in the right place, for I sought the Kingdom first. Yet the entire time Mickey and I were fulfilling God's directives, I literally battled against demonic spirits of murmuring, complaining, selfish desires, lusts of the flesh, doubt and fear. I could find absolutely no joy at all. It was almost as if every thought that surfaced gained a seated position in my life. Negativity had come knocking, and I should not have answered the door!

Chronic Dissatisfaction, Idolatry and Pride

During this blessing that I could see only as a crisis, I also began to battle against a lustful desire for more. Chronic dissatisfaction and idolatry had overtaken me because I had opened the door to Mammon, who was trying to take me captive.

You see, when Mammon is involved we develop an ungodly need to "compete with the Joneses." We begin to covet, and

vinces us to buy more things in order to appear
el acceptable to others. This evil spirit tells us
ss than" if we do not have designer handbags or
expensive automobiles. If we are not cautious, we can easily
be seduced into believing that we need more, more and more!
Before we know it, we have fallen into Mammon's trap.

I was up against a major death structure. A death structure is erected when we are controlled by our sinful natures.
Ephesians 2:12 states that apart from Christ we are "without
hope and without God" and "controlled by the sinful nature" (Romans 7:5). We therefore become slaves of Satan (see
2 Timothy 2:26). I was being controlled by my own sinful
nature, and in allowing that I had opened the door to Mammon, a spirit of bondage. I had fallen into the snares of the
enemy, and because I had not allowed Jesus to fulfill all my
needs, I had acquired a sense of spiritual bankruptcy.

And the irony was that all this time I was writing a book
on the spirit of Mammon! Indeed, the very same spirit
that God had told me to expose in a book was attacking
me full force. As I was writing on Mammon, I was warring against him. The deception of Mammon became a
personal battle for me.

Lord, I prayed, *will You ever allow me to write a book
that does not require baring every part of my life? Talk
about taking up my cross and following You! I know it is
important to be real—but really! Can You please just allow
me to write a book or article that is flowery and sunny for
a change instead of my baring my entire soul for everyone
to know my life challenges?* As you can see, dear reader,
God did not answer this prayer.

I soon realized that pride was involved. After all, it is
pride that causes us to compare ourselves to others. I did
not even realize pride was in my heart until we moved to

116

the country. Previously we had lived in a beautiful neighbor-hood with manicured lawns and gardens. In the country there are, of course, no manicured lawns—in fact, I had to forget about manicures in every way. It was miles to the nail salon or even to the grocery store. I was embarrassed about my lawn, embarrassed about my nails, and I continued to let my pride rule me as I murmured and complained.

My spoiled rotten attitude was ridiculous and ungodly. I had little energy to work on the ranch because I was using all of my energy to murmur. I was tired every day because I ran my mouth all day long. It became exhausting, I can assure you. And most importantly, it greatly displeased God.

I am amazed at how quickly Mammon can move in and take over a person's thoughts and life. For me, it truly began with dissatisfaction. It was so hidden in my heart that I did not realize it was there. Not yet confronted by God's finger of deliverance, the dissatisfaction mushroomed into alarming levels of *chronic* dissatisfaction, which is linked to a spirit of whoredoms. The spirit of whoredoms is linked to spiritual adultery, which is connected to idolatry. Mam-mon is an idol, remember? He seeks to be worshiped, and chronic dissatisfaction leads us directly into bowing down to him.

Within six months of our move, I was a stressed mess. I was dissatisfied, worried about money, concerned for our financial future, feeling pressure to have more money and wanting to move back to the city—which, by the way, would be disobedient and "going back to Egypt." All in all, I desired a financial "treasure" rather than the true treasure of being obedient and faithful to our godly assignment.

You see, God has given Mickey and me a dream that is as yet unfulfilled. He has given us a vision for and a desire to operate a Kingdom Training Center—that is, a place that exists for the glory of promoting God's Kingdom. Our hearts are pointed toward Kingdom training with joint community efforts to empower others. We desire to have dormitories, houses for unwed mothers and their newborns, a convalescent facility and a retirement community—all Christ-based. This godly vision is the treasure we seek, and the enemy has been attempting to twist and pervert my heart since the day God began to bless us financially because he does not want this God-given vision to come to fruition. He was using the spirit of Mammon to direct me down a wrong path.

Treasures

My problem was that I was treasuring other things above God. Our hearts can become perverted if we treasure anything above our relationship with Him.

> Lay not up for yourselves treasures upon the earth, where moth and rust consume, and where thieves break through and steal: but lay up for yourselves treasures in heaven, where neither moth nor rust doth consume, and where thieves do not break through nor steal: *for where thy treasure is, there will thy heart be also.*
>
> Matthew 6:19–21, ASV, emphasis added

Did you get that? Jesus said that whatever is in our hearts is our treasure.

What is *treasure* anyway? The Greek word for *treasure* in this passage is *thesaurus*, which means "a deposit or wealth."[1] It is connected to another Greek word, *thesauros,* a place in which "goods and precious things are collected and laid up."[2]

You see, we can "collect" attitudes in our hearts—such as love of money, fear of not having money, greediness, selfishness, etc.—and then "lay up" these attitudes for a period of time. Out of these heart attitudes—or "treasure"—false belief systems begin to manifest. What has been collected in our hearts becomes exposed.

Further inspection of the Greek translation reveals that *treasure* can be a "casket" where valuables are kept.[3] Talk about a death structure! Wrong heart motives about a treasure can bury us prematurely. This is why these false belief systems must be torn down. Indeed, we cannot allow any area of our hearts to be seduced by Mammon or the evil seductions of spiritual idolatry.

When I think of hidden treasure, I think of treasure chests filled with jewels, gold and precious pearls and buried in the sand beneath miles of seawater just waiting to be discovered. In a spiritual sense, our treasure often is hidden from us until God later reveals it. Jesus even told a parable about the treasures buried deep within us. True treasures are realized through hardships, seeking God for answers and needing breakthroughs.

What seemed unimportant at one time becomes priceless when it is lost. I can remember not valuing a certain relationship until that relationship was gone. If I had considered that relationship a treasure, then I would have valued it more. It is the same with our relationship with God.

Often in difficulty we turn our hearts away from God. We are encouraged, however, in 2 Corinthians 4:1–12 to faint not, renounce sin and preach not ourselves, but Christ Jesus. In other words, we are to build God's Kingdom and not our own. And though we may be persecuted, we are to know that "we have this treasure in earthen vessels, that the excellency of the power may be of God, and not of us" (verse 7, KJV). The passage goes on to say:

> We are troubled on every side, yet not distressed; we are perplexed, but not in despair; persecuted, but not forsaken; cast down, but not destroyed; always bearing about in the body the dying of the Lord Jesus, that the life also of Jesus might be made manifest in our body. For we which live are always delivered unto death for Jesus' sake, that the life also of Jesus might be made manifest in our mortal flesh. So then death worketh in us, but life in you.
>
> verses 8–12, KJV

If we only treasure God for the good times, then we will miss it! God never guaranteed us all the money in the world, wealth beyond imagination, or a lack of misfortune. He does desire and even promise to bless us, but we must also realize that our hearts will be tested. Whatever we treasure in our hearts will go through the fire.

Our hearts, then, are treasure chests that are "hidden" and later "found." If we treasure the wrong things, then we are disappointed when that treasure chest is finally opened. But if we store up godly riches, then those precious truths and revelations concerning God's Kingdom are there at just the right time when we need that treasure. We open up the chest to find that our wealth is great, and we have all we need.

Our hearts, therefore, need to be ready to receive His revelation. We need to treasure the spiritual truths God gives us. If we focus on Him and the richness of knowing Him, then all other things (money, wealth, etc.) will be added. But first our hearts must be aligned with His perfect will. Our hearts are to be a treasure chest of truth, and then He can trust us with other riches.

Is Achan in Our Hearts?

> But the children of Israel committed a trespass in the *accursed thing*: for Achan, the son of Carmi, the son of Zabdi, the son of Zerah, of the tribe of Judah, took of the *accursed thing*: and the anger of the LORD was kindled against the children of Israel.
>
> Joshua 7:1, KJV, emphasis added

Joshua 7 describes how Joshua led a battle against the city of Ai with a handful of warriors because it was considered an "easy take." Joshua sent three thousand men into Ai, a Canaanite city, to ransack it, take its spoils and offer everything to God. It should have been an easy victory. Instead the battle was lost and Joshua's men fled before the army of Ai, which chased the dispirited Israelite warriors away in total humiliation.

What went wrong? Joshua sought God for an answer to this question and was alerted that one man, Achan, had taken the "accursed things"—spoils that were to be dedicated totally to God. Motivated by Mammon, Achan had taken a Babylonian garment and Canaanite money and buried them. Since God had directed the Israelites to dedicate *all* of the spoils to Him, Achan's act was sinful. God told Joshua, "There is an accursed thing in the midst of you, and therefore sanctify yourselves." In other words, one man had sinned, causing all Israel to require sanctification.

When Joshua approached Achan, the thief confessed:

121

When I *saw* among the spoils a goodly Babylonish garment, and two hundred shekels of silver, and a wedge of gold of fifty shekels weight, then I *coveted* them, and *took* them; and, behold, they are *hid* in the earth in the midst of my tent, and the silver under it.

Joshua 7:21, KJV, emphasis added

Achan's response reveals three things that we should guard against when battling against Mammon and the evil influence of Babylon:

1. Achan *saw* the spoils. We should be careful, then, not to focus on the ungodly wealth of the world. If we *see* it as good, then we will *covet*.
2. Achan *coveted*. Coveting is a sin, and sin places us in bondage. If we covet, then we allow ourselves to become slaves to Satan. Whatever we *covet* empowers us to *take*.
3. Achan *took* the spoils that really belonged to God and *hid* them. Taking is also *partaking*. If we *covet*, then we *partake* of evil, and eventually we attempt to *hide* things from others and from God. An example of this would be hiding or hoarding money and not giving God what belongs to Him.

God says that whatever is hidden will be revealed. Achan had a heart issue—he suffered from the sin connected to Mammon and Babylon. He was a slave to Satan.

It is the same for us today. This evil stronghold, Mammon, deceives us into lusting after "garments"—things that should be devoted unto God. Until we pray to bring down this Babylonian god, which is so prevalent in our midst, then we will not be victorious against our enemy.

God desires to entrust us with His treasures. As He begins to examine our hearts, will He find that He can trust us?

Achan had to be put to death along with his family and then burned with fire:

> Joshua, together with all Israel, took Achan son of Zerah, the silver, the robe, the gold wedge, his sons and daughters, his cattle, donkeys and sheep, his tent and all that he had, to the Valley of Achor. . . . Then all Israel stoned him, and after they had stoned the rest, they burned them. Over Achan they heaped up a large pile of rocks, which remains to this day. Then the LORD turned from his fierce anger. Therefore that place has been called the Valley of Achor ever since.
>
> Joshua 7:24–26

Achan's demise reveals the death structure that is built when we seek Babylon and the "accursed things." If Babylon is in our hearts as we war for God's Kingdom, then we will be tempted to take the spoils and not give God His portion. Dear ones, when this happens, death develops, and it must be cleansed with God's holy fire!

The Valley of Achor

Joshua 7 says that the place where Achan was stoned was called the Valley of Achor. *Achor* translates "troubled."[4] Why did the Israelites name this "the Valley of the Troubled"?

According to the *Miriam-Webster Online Dictionary*, *trouble* means "worry, disturb, mistreat, oppress, afflict, be at pains, to be inconvenienced (I am sorry to *trouble* you)."[5] It also is connected to the word *turbulent*.

Jesus said that we are never to worry or be "troubled" about tomorrow. To be concerned about the future is not

123

to trust God. The spirit behind the fear for our future is Mammon—plain and simple. My testimony concerning my struggles is a clear example of one being troubled over money and a lack of trust in God's ability to provide for my every need.

The Greek word for *worry* is *merimnao*, which stems from the words *merizo* ("divide") and *nous* ("mind").[6] Worry divides our minds in such a way that we become double-minded. James 1:8 states that a double-minded man is unstable in all his ways. When we are unstable, we lose the sure-footed faith we have in God's ability to protect our days and provide our daily bread. Mammon again! Since double-mindedness also means division and disunity, it is impossible to be in unity with God's Word, believing His promises of provision. Mammon is sneaky. Be on guard against double-mindedness, or else Mammon will attempt to beguile you.

Achan, then, was troubled because he did not trust in God's provision for him and his family. Indeed, we all are a troubled people when our hearts are bent toward the Babylonian system. My daddy always said, "Trouble follows troubled hearts." I believe this is true. When our hearts are troubled, it opens the door to more trouble. If we will just learn to rest in God, to know Him and trust Him, then trouble will not have a place.

The Spirit of Canaan

Ai was a Canaanite city, and since the biblical land of Canaan is representative of our spiritual Promised Land, it is important for us to take a look at the Canaanites and the spirit behind them. In addition, we need to focus on how this stronghold affects us today.

The spirit of Canaan is closely associated with Mammon, and the two work together. The word *Canaan* in Hebrew is translated as "merchant, trader and trafficker." It also means "to be brought low, humbled or under subjection."[7] Most of us are keen to the idea that Satan wants to bring us low and under his subjection, but have we realized it might be through the bondage of Mammon?

Alongside the Canaanite spirit, Mammon seeks an exalted position in our lives. In Johnny Enlowe's insightful book, *The Seven Mountain Prophecy*, he says, "Mammon wrestles for God's seat in your life. . . . He [Mammon] tells you he is actually your source for all true provision, and therefore for all peace and happiness. He is so deceptive and his web is so intriguing that most of us are caught up in it to some degree."[8] Enlowe proceeds to imply, as have I, that Mammon's influence manifests often as greed and selfishness.

These false belief systems promoted by Mammon set us on a cyclical course. We are afraid of being poor, so we hoard things. Hoarding produces greed, and greed produces poverty. Poverty, then, promotes more greed. Partaking of one evil simply leads to another evil, until eventually we end up at the same place we started. Dear ones, we must understand that the Canaanite spirits of greed and poverty oppose God's promises of Kingdom provision and Kingdom living.

Mammon seduces us into not trusting God, into relying on government for financial assistance when we are perfectly capable of working, and into looking at "trade" and "merchants" as the answers to our problems. Dear ones, the only trade that is truly sanctified is the trade Jesus made at the cross: His blood for my sins and sorrows. I am not advocating that all trade is evil. Rather, I am saying it is a matter of the heart. I can trade in the stock market, but I need to stay focused on the fact that the market is not my god. My God reigns over stocks, trading, Wall Street and the economy. It is the attitude and motive of the heart about which God is concerned. Ask yourself this: Am I controlled by a Canaanite spirit, a spirit of Mammon or God's Holy Spirit? On whom am I relying?

Treasures Hidden in a Field

You see, dear ones, God wants us to be traders and merchants in His Kingdom. That is the trade He is most concerned with. In Matthew 13:44–45 Jesus said, "The kingdom of heaven is like a treasure hidden in the field. . . . The kingdom of heaven is like a merchant seeking fine pearls"(NASB). Notice again the words *treasure* and *merchant*. As we seek His Kingdom, we must be as merchants or traders seeking treasure or beautiful pearls. God does not want us to be Babylon's merchants and traders. Rather, He wants us to serve with pure hearts so that we can be His vessels against the spirit of Mammon.

This passage also makes me think of how the prophet Ezekiel prophesied to dry bones buried in the earth—he had a resurrection service in the Valley of Dry Bones! An entire army was resurrected, and life was breathed into them.

My prophetic gifting empowers me to see hidden treasure—thank God! Yet when seeking His Kingdom, I should be as a merchant seeking beautiful pearls.

Where to Lay Up Your Treasure

> Lay not up for yourselves treasures upon earth, where moth and rust doth corrupt, and where thieves break through and steal.
>
> Matthew 6:19, KJV

126

In ancient times pagan people buried gold, silver, gems, wine, lands, houses and oil along with their dead. How many of us are basically doing the same thing today in a spiritual sense when we hoard things and trust in them rather than trusting in God? We are not to lay up (store) treasures where moth and rust corrupt and where thieves can break in and steal.

The theologian Albert Barnes said, "When a Hebrew or Orientalist spoke of wealth, they first thought of what would make a 'display,' and included as an essential part splendid articles of dress. . . . The 'moth' is a small insect that finds its way to clothes and garments and destroys them. The 'moth' would destroy their apparel, the 'rust' their silver and gold; thus, all their treasure would waste away. The word rendered 'rust' signifies anything that 'eats into,' and hence, anything that would consume one's property, and may have a wider signification than mere rust."[9]

Where your treasure is, there your heart is also. If your heart, therefore, is bent toward the world and you covet what is in the world, then the enemy can break in and steal from you. Our protection from the thief is to treasure our relationship with God and know that He is all we truly need in life. He is the source of true joy. Dear ones, lay up your treasure in Him.

Our Daily Bread

God directs us quite clearly to trust Him with our daily provision. Each day is new and deserves a fresh start, and God expects us daily to ask Him to "give us this day our daily bread." When we do so, it releases us from controlling our day. Of course, we need to work and be diligent, but we are to cast the daily provision onto God's shoulders. God wants us to depend upon Him completely. If we do not, then we are carrying a burden that He does not intend for us to carry, and the result is dead works and perfectionism.

Matthew Henry says, "We may ask for temporal things if we ask for them lawfully." I agree with his statement. If it is in God's will and His Word, then we should ask—and ask in faith. We cannot, however, take Scripture out of context and ask for *anything*—our hearts need to be aligned with His timing and will. We also must ask with humility and submission and never with vain imaginations, for that would be asking out of the influence of Mammon.

The Door of Hope

Let's do a quick study of Hosea 2:15–20 (KJV):

> And I will give her her vineyards from thence, and the valley of Achor for a door of hope: and she shall sing there, as in the days of her youth, and as in the day when she came up out of the land of Egypt. And it shall be at that day, saith the LORD, that thou shalt call me Ishi; and shalt call me no more Baali. For I will take away the names of Baalim out of her mouth, and they shall no more be remembered by their name. And in that day will I make a covenant for them with the beasts of the field and with the fowls of heaven, and with the creeping things of the ground: and I will break the bow and the sword and the battle out of the earth, and will make them to lie down safely. And I will betroth thee unto me for ever; yea, I will betroth thee unto me in righteousness, and in judgment, and in loving-kindness, and in mercies. I will even betroth thee unto me in faithfulness: and thou shalt know the LORD.

What an encouraging passage! It says that instead of your experiencing constant trouble, God will:

1. Give you vineyards.
2. Turn your valley of Achor (trouble) into a door of hope.
3. Make you to sing as in the times you were delivered from Egypt (deliverance).
4. Make covenant with you.
5. Marry you for all eternity in His righteousness and justice.
6. Cause you to *know* the Lord (be intimate with Him).

Dear ones, isn't that great? God wants to turn your valley of trouble into a door of hope. It is a promise of provision. You are His treasure, and He desires to be yours.

Now, let me ask you again: Where is your treasure? I encourage you to seek the Holy Spirit regarding what may be hidden in your heart. Then stop and let God know how much you desire to be with Him, know Him and understand His perfect will for your life. He is waiting for you.

Birthing a Promise

Well, I must tell you that I eventually was victorious in my personal battle with Mammon. And the Lord birthed a promise in me.

It was a delightful spring evening; yet Mickey and I could see an imminent storm approaching from miles away. We sat on our ranch patio with our eyes fixed on our horse stables and the apparent changing weather patterns. We anxiously awaited some sign that Chelsea, our five-year-old thoroughbred, was about to deliver her foal. As soon as we knew she was expecting, we became excited. The eleven-month wait, however, led to concern as well as excited anticipation, since many mares had been carrying their babies past full term, endangering the lives of mother and foal.

Several nights earlier we had helped two friends hand deliver a colt from the womb. This was an experience beyond description, and one that was most rewarding. The birth had taken an hour and a half, with two men literally pulling the colt from its mother's womb. The delivery wreaked havoc on the mother, ripping and tearing her womb, but thankfully no surgery was required. I remember praying earnestly during the delivery, *Lord, You know how to empower us to help this mother. Protect both baby and mom.* And He did! The mother experienced some aftershock and needed some mending, but medications and some TLC healed her body and spirit. The colt, by the way, was perfectly healthy. I decided, however, that I did not want to experience that trauma with Chelsea.

My struggle with Mammon had been long and hard, and the birth of our friends' mare seemed symbolic of what I knew the Lord was birthing in me. I felt a new day approaching, but I still was in the middle of the "storm" in my life—my battle against Mammon.

Watching Chelsea pace back and forth caused me to be concerned. *It is getting close now. Lord, don't let her have her baby during the storm.* I knew there was nothing more troubling than to deliver a mare in rain, snow or sleet.

Within minutes lightning was flashing, rain poured down in sheets, the wind blew hard and steady, and all of our horses were jumping and kicking in fear. Chelsea jumped around more than I had seen her move in months. *Lord! Protect Chelsea and her baby!* The rain was so thick that I could not see my hand in front of my face. I panicked. "Mickey! Can you see the horses at all?"

Suddenly the wind, rain and lightning stopped. *Thank You, Lord!*

"I see her," Mickey responded. "She is standing by the fence."

As I turned toward the pasture to look for her, my eyes fell upon the most beautiful rainbow I had ever seen. Stretched across our 54 acres, it seemed so close that I could have run out to touch it. "Look, Mickey, a rainbow! Grab the camera, quick!"

That rainbow elevated my faith to a blue-ribbon status. I was immersed in its wonder. The colors perfectly formed a bow of delight, and it seemed to shine pure love upon us. Knowing the rainbow is a symbol of God's covenant, I considered it a sign of encouragement from Him. As Mickey and I watched this sign of God's promises stretched out across our property, we both were moved by the awesome power of our God and touched by His covenant upon our land. Up to that moment neither of us realized how important it was that we witness that rainbow. We were touched, humbled and in complete awe as we basked in God's beauty reaching from the sky.

My hard struggle with Mammon was coming to an end. God was reiterating His promises to Mickey and me. We had followed Him to the country, and He was blessing us. I knew I could release Chelsea, our new home and our lives to Him.

God was right on time with His divine encouragement.

6

Is There an Ammonite in Your Treasury?

And I . . . understood of the evil that Eliashib did for Tobiah, in preparing him a chamber in the courts of the house of God. And it grieved me sore: therefore I cast forth all the household stuff to Tobiah out of the chamber. Then I commanded, and they cleansed the chambers: and thither brought I again the vessels of the house of God, with the meat offering and the frankincense.

Nehemiah 13:7–9, KJV

Few of us have read the book of Nehemiah in its entirety. While we may know, therefore, that Nehemiah was a godly prophet who was responsible for rebuilding the walls of Jerusalem, most of us are not aware of the fact that the priests allowed Tobiah, the ungodly, unholy, demonically inspired enemy of Israel, to move into God's treasury room and possess it. This biblical account is important because it is a physical representation of a spiritual truth: We do not want to allow our enemy to move in and take over our hearts and lives, so we must heed the warning of this account. We must refuse to allow any "room" for an Ammonite spirit that seeks to take over our hearts.

Let's start with the account of Nehemiah.

The Season to Rebuild What Was Torn Down

It was the month of December. Nehemiah stood overlooking the palace walls. *Shushan is lovely this time of year*, he thought. He gazed at the palace hangings, sparkling with their violet threads and fabrics, which were available for viewing during the winter. For years the ancient palace had been the winter residence of Persian kings, and Nehemiah was taking in its splendor. *Still, it's not Jerusalem,* Nehemiah sighed. *How I long to be in my own homeland!*

Shushan was one of the oldest known settlements and possibly was founded as early as 4200 BC. Its ancient city walls towered over its surroundings and boasted of its bulwark tenacity to endure history and captivate many kings, for it had been sought after by many empires. Nehemiah had no idea that soon Queen Esther would be positioned in the exact same palace to shift a death decree made against the Jews. He also had no way of knowing that King Cyrus would also be there and give him permission to rebuild the Temple of Jerusalem. Indeed, much history unfolded in the place where Nehemiah stood.

It was the time of the Babylonian captivity of Israel. The Jews had been exiled to Babylon by Nebuchadnezzar II in 586 BC. It was the most traumatic event in Jewish history, as the destruction of their political independence coincided with the destruction of their Temple in Jerusalem. Yet, though the Jews were in captivity, they continued to develop their faith and practice their religious traditions. It was, however, always in their hearts to return to Jerusalem. This was the greatest desire of Nehemiah's heart.

"Nehemiah! . . . Nehemiah!" He was so engulfed in his own thoughts of returning to his homeland that it took two calls before he heard the messenger.

"I'm over here."

"Someone named Hanani is here with others to see you. I believe they said they were from . . . um . . . is it Judah? Do you recognize the name of the place? If not, I will quickly send them away."

"Did you say they were from Judah? Why, yes! Send them here!" Nehemiah was bursting with excitement. He could hardly wait to inquire about how things were going in Jerusalem.

"My friends! How is Jerusalem? How is everyone there getting along? Have the Jews who returned to Jerusalem from exile come here with you?" Nehemiah was so full of questions that the visitors could not respond quickly enough.

Sadly Hanani's report concerning the condition of his countrymen was not good. "Well," Hanani said, "the remnant who were left there are in great affliction. The walls are torn down, and the gates have been burned."

"Stop!" Nehemiah raised his hand. "No more." Nehemiah turned and walked away to grieve in private. His heart was crushed. He fought hatred, sorrow and grief all at the same time. He was unable to eat for days and spent much time in prayer for his people.

"O God, the God who keeps His promises and is so loving and kind to those who truly love and obey Him, please hear my prayer! Listen closely to what I say and please look down and see me praying night and day for Your people, Israel. I am burdened for them. I confess that I have sinned against You, and yes, my people have committed the horrible sin of disobedience. But please remember what You told Moses. You said, 'If you sin, I will scatter you among the nations; but if you return to Me and obey My laws, even though you are exiled to the farthest corners of the universe, I will bring you back to Jerusalem. For Jerusalem is the place in which I have chosen to live.' We are Your servants and Your people who have been used by Your hand and Your own power. Please heed the prayers of one who honors You. Help me now as I go and ask the king for great favor—put it in his heart to be kind to me. Let me move in Your timing to utter my request to the king. Let Your favor rest upon me, my Lord" (see Nehemiah 1:8).

Nehemiah was the king's cupbearer. At each meal he would pour the king's wine and taste it before the king did to ensure that no one was poisoning the king. The king, therefore, had great trust in Nehemiah, and Nehemiah daily was positioned quite close to the king. The two talked often.

Four months after Hanani's visit, Nehemiah was serving the king his wine when the ruler asked Nehemiah, "Why do you look so sad? Are you sick or troubled? You have always seemed cheerful, but now—something must be wrong."

Nehemiah, knowing he must use wisdom with his words, prayed silently for favor to share his heartache with the king and then replied reverently, "Why shouldn't I be sad? The city where my ancestors are buried is in ruins and the gates are burned down."

"Well, what can be done?" The king handed his wine glass back to Nehemiah for refilling.

"If it pleases Your Majesty and if you look upon me with your royal favor, then please send me to Judah. It is in my heart to rebuild the city of my fathers."

The king glanced at his queen, who sat beside him— both shared the same compassion for Nehemiah and cared deeply for him. "How long will you be away? When can you return?"

It was agreed that Nehemiah would soon depart. Before leaving the room, he took a deep breath and requested one more thing: "If it pleases the king, give me letters to those who govern west of the Euphrates River and instruct them to let me travel through their countries. I also request a letter to Asaph, the manager of your forest, instructing him to give timber for the gates of the fortress near the Temple, as well as the city walls— and of course, a house for myself." The king graciously nodded his head.

What favor my God has given to me! Nehemiah recognized the Lord's faithfulness.

When Nehemiah passed through the provinces west of the river, he delivered the letters to the governors. He made quite an impression on them because the king had sent an army of officers and troops to protect him. In addition, he brought with him loads of timber and other building materials given by the king, as well as builders, craftsmen and laborers. It was quite a caravan. How God divinely protected and provided for Nehemiah as this righteous man took a leap of faith and believed God for a miracle.

Indeed, Nehemiah was God's obedient vessel who acted in faith and was led by God's Spirit to rebuild the walls of Jerusalem. Unfortunately this did not stop the plans of Satan, who continually opposed Nehemiah. When Sanballat, the Horonite, Tobiah, an Ammonite and governmental official, and Geshem, an Arab, heard that Nehemiah was commissioned to help Israel, they were angry and set their hearts to stop him. Sanballat and Tobiah were used by Satan to oppose God's building plans.

And so the battle between good and evil began again. It is the same battle we face today. God wants to rebuild each of our lives, and we face an enemy who seeks to destroy us.

Sanballat, Tobiah and Geshem

After Nehemiah returned to Jerusalem, he went out during the night and inspected the city. He later gathered the city officials, religious leaders and others and said, "Let us rebuild the wall of Jerusalem and rid ourselves of this disgrace!" (Nehemiah 2:17, TLB). The inhabitants of Jerusalem rejoiced at the thought of rebuilding. Sanballat and Tobiah, however, along with Geshem, scoffed at their plans. But Nehemiah put his faith in God and condemned their lack of faith. "The God of heaven will help us," he boldly declared.

Sanballat and Tobiah are historically noted for attempting to discourage Nehemiah. In fact, they were relentless in their pursuit to discourage him. They were angry, enraged and insulted, and they mocked Nehemiah and those at the wall. Yet Geshem, too, is the often-overlooked opposition, and we will look at all three because they complete a threefold demonic cord. The spiritual aspect of a threefold demonic cord is so important that I actually wrote an entire book on the subject: *Breaking the Threefold Demonic Cord.*

> As we pull down strongholds and demonic powers, we need to be aware of the threefold cord the enemy uses against us. . . . The use of a triple braided cord, or rope, dates backs thousands of years. . . . A rope with only two strands is not nearly as strong as a rope with three. The strength of only two cords is unpredictable, but adding an additional cord proves an almost invincible might.[1]

The Lord said, "A threefold cord is not quickly broken" (Ecclesiastes 4:12, KJV). I believe Satan planned to use these three particular men as a threefold, demonically inspired cord to halt Nehemiah's plans.

The name *Sanballat* translates "hate in disguise; the enemy is secret; a hidden branch; hatred (or throne) in secret."[2] This name embodies the fact that the enemy attempts to remain hidden while seeking a seated position in our lives. Satan does not like exposure.

Tobiah means "Jehovah is good." It also means "distinguished of the Lord."[3] Tobiah, however, never embraced his potential to be used by God. As we examine his name, let's take a deeper look into our own hearts and ask a question: How often have we overlooked our own potential in the Lord and instead been scoffers and mocked God's building plans? I have to admit that I have made this mistake. I have quickly judged a particular church building project and did not believe the church was following God. Perhaps Mammon was at work in my own heart.

How many of us have seen a church expanding, adding walls or a new building, and declared, "What are they doing? Why are they expanding? We do not need another church on the block—there are enough churches in town already. This is just another money project. I am so tired of building programs and churches raising money!" Dear ones, usually this is the voice of Tobiah, which hinders God's divine building process. And yes, Satan will attempt to use us to oppose God's building plans!

Geshem, the name of the third adversary of Nehemiah, means "to rain or cause to rain."[4] To me this means that the enemy keeps trying to rain on my parade. He certainly attempted it with Nehemiah as he continuously concurred with the attitudes of Sanballat and Tobiah. Have you ever felt that the devil keeps bringing a rainstorm when you need sunshine? If you have ever attempted to build something for God—a ministry, church, church project, etc.—and others scoff at your building plan and rain on your parade, then you can join the club of Nehemiah. We are all in the same boat if we are truly building God's Kingdom.

Why were these three opponents so angry? Was it because it involved the Jews? Well, perhaps somewhat, but I do not believe this was the full picture. Remember that the king gave Nehemiah his favor and materials to build—in essence, great riches. When someone else is blessed with favor and wealth, many of us experience competition, jealousy, anger and strife. If we notice someone else being blessed and our knee-jerk reaction is envy, then you can bet Mammon is punching his time clock and going to work.

We all have opposed God's plans at one time or another. In doing so, we have allowed the spirits of Mammon and Babylon to have power over our lives. Mammon is seductive, and we often swallow his hook before realizing it. Soon we end up "caught" like a deer in the headlights—and Mammon is exposed.

The Plain of Ono

When Sanballat, Tobiah, Geshem and the rest of Nehemiah's enemies discovered that Nehemiah and the Israelites had almost completed the building project, they sent a message requesting that Nehemiah meet them on the Plain of Ono. They could not believe that Nehemiah had accomplished his task and probably felt like failures for not frustrating his plans. They were jealous, contentious, angry and irritated that Jerusalem had been rebuilt and that so many resources (money) had been used.

Nehemiah had great discernment and realized they were probably trying to kill him. Thank God, he did not fall into their seductive trap. Four times they sent the same message, and each time Nehemiah gave them the same answer: "I am carrying on a great project and cannot go down. Why should the work stop while I leave it and go down to you?" In other words, "Satan, you will not stop me from carrying on the work of God."

A fifth time Sanballat sent his aide to Nehemiah with the same message in letter form, requesting again that he meet them on the Plain of Ono. This letter accused Nehemiah of leading a revolt of the Jews, planning to be their king and even appointing prophets to a kingship position. They once again requested that Nehemiah meet to confer with them. Yet again Nehemiah discerned that they were deceitful and lay in wait to murder him. He held his ground and prayed for God to strengthen his hands to continue to build, then again declared a firm "no" to the death structure of Mammon.

Mammon seeks to cause us to become double-minded, which means a person is not in unity with God and His purpose for his or her life. Nehemiah, however, refused to go to the Plain of Ono. He believed in God's purpose and remained steadfast. The result? Jerusalem was rebuilt and a total of 42,360 citizens returned to Judah, along with numerous slaves and animals. Many of them gave gifts of gold and silver to the building project as they returned home during the month of September.

In mid-September, Ezra, their priest, was requested to read the law in front of the Water Gate. He brought out the scroll of Moses' Laws, stood on a wooden stand and read from early morning until noon. Everyone was filled with joy. The Israelites entered a season of repentance, cleansing and agreement never to allow the Temple of God to be neglected again.

More and more people moved back to Jerusalem from the different territories. The priesthood began to grow, and soon 284 Levites (priests) and 172 gatekeepers dwelled in Jerusalem, along with many merchants. The Holy City had come back to life and was booming once again.

There Is a Thief in the Treasury!

Soon the priests dedicated the city wall. It was an incredible event! Cymbals, psalteries, harps and singing resounded in praise to God as they dedicated the wall to Him. Sacrifices were made, women rejoiced and children danced. That same day men were appointed to be in charge of the treasuries, wave offerings, tithes and first-of-the-harvest offerings.

Also on that same day, the people found in the Law of Moses a rule that the Ammonites and Moabites were never to be permitted to worship at the Temple, for they had come into agreement with Balaam, the false prophet influenced by Mammon. No foreigners, therefore, especially the Ammonites and Moabites, were allowed in the Temple. When the rule was read, all foreigners were immediately expelled from the assembly.

Eliashib, however, the priest who was a custodian of the Temple and a good friend of Tobiah—an Ammonite—had converted the treasury of the Temple into a room in which Tobiah was allowed to live. Did you get that? The priesthood itself allowed the enemy into the treasury! Right in the place where tithes were stored, the thief was allowed to live. Eliashib's name, by the way, means "whom God restores; whom God leads back again; God will restore; God is requiter; God has restored." Eliashib was a priest restored by God and was to oversee what was restored by God, yet he let the enemy into the heart of the financial structure of the Temple.

When Nehemiah discovered this abomination—along with some others committed by the Israelites—he took immediate action. He threw out all of Tobiah's belongings and cleansed the room and the Temple. He replaced what had been taken away, bringing back the Temple bowls and grain offerings. He restored divine order.

How quickly the Israelites forgot the voice of their enemy! The very one who opposed their building, their restoration and their prosperity was allowed entrance into their storehouse. Are we that easily seduced today? How can we cleanse the temple of our hearts if we have allowed the enemy to strip us, seduce us and defile our lives? Embracing Mammon or any influence of Satan causes great affliction, reproach, ruin and wreckage. Yet God empowered Nehemiah to perform a ministry of encouragement to the people. After leading them in rebuilding the physical Temple, he also encouraged them and helped them to rebuild the spiritual temple.

Do you need rebuilding today? Has Mammon robbed you of your joy and stolen your treasure? If Mammon is ruling, then you are in bondage. If the enemy has torn down your walls, then you will face opposition as you seek to heal and rebuild. Let us not be sidetracked. Let us be like Nehemiah and remain on task to restore God's divine order.

Mammon and Ammon

Note that Tobiah was an Ammonite. The name *Ammon* is derived from the word *Mammon*.[5] When we read about the Ammonites, therefore, we are also reading about the influence of Mammon. What does it mean, then, to allow an Ammonite into the treasury of our hearts?

We must recognize the seductiveness of Mammon and Babylon and how they link up with an Ammonite stronghold not only to steal our treasure, but also to totally possess it. In other words, Mammon seeks to steal and harden our hearts. Believe me, there is nothing the enemy wants more than our hearts. He wants to totally possess the "room" of our hearts and cause us to fall away from our first Love. Remember that where our hearts are, there also is our treasure. If we have a deep love of money, then Satan is beguiling us and seducing us from the truth. Dear ones, we must guard our hearts.

A quick biblical study of the Ammonites reveals the destruction that comes to those who align themselves in any way with this stronghold:

1. The Ammonite wives seduced Solomon into idolatry.
2. The Ammonite Molech was an idolater who made child sacrifices to his false god. This is the same

144

stronghold that is behind abortion, and it also is connected to a Jezebel spirit.

3. The Ammonites and those who allow that spirit entrance are cursed to the tenth generation (see Deuteronomy 23:3).

4. The king of the Ammonites was Milcom (see 1 Kings 11:33). In many circumstances Milcom was called "Molech," the king who sacrificed children to his false god. *Milcom* translates "great king" and "crown." This translation speaks to the fact that Satan attempts to be crowned king over our lives and futures and to remain in a seated position of authority over our lives.

5. According to Zephaniah 1:5 (AMP), the spirit of Molech causes us to serve God only in words and not in deeds. In other words, we acknowledge that we know God with our mouths, but do not truly know Him in our hearts.

Precious believers, as I continue to write I feel more and more convicted. I have bowed my knee to the enemy's schemes and believed his lies—especially when under financial pressure. I have allowed the Ammonite spirit into the room of my heart. Have you?

I want Jesus to reign in my heart. I want Him to rule in and through me.

A Prayer of Praise and Repentance

If you feel you want to examine your heart and spend some quality time with the Lord, then I have written a prayer for you. Know that I have already prayed for you even before you received this book—and I am praying again as I write it.

Father, I thank You for being a God who truly watches over us 24/7. You are my fortress and high tower. I run to You! According to Psalm 35, I ask that You contend with those who contend with me and You fight against all evil that fights against me. I ask that You take up shield and buckler and arise to come to my aid. Put to shame all enemies who seek my life and plot my ruin. As the enemy sets snares for me, I stand strong in my belief that You will alert me to the traps that have been set for my destruction. Lord, You know my heart. Search every area that needs cleansing. As Your light shines into the deep crevices, allow exposure to come so that I may repent and be free.

(Take a few moments now to be silent and ask the Lord to speak to you concerning any hidden sin or motive.)

I repent for the sin of (write below the areas where you need to repent):

I break any covenant with the Ammonite stronghold that has attempted to rule over my finances and belief systems concerning money and wealth. I ask that You forgive me for giving place to the enemy. I forgive my ancestors and my generations for allowing sin to have a seated position in their lives. Cleanse me from all unrighteousness and cover me with the precious blood of Christ Jesus.

I declare that there is none like You, O mighty God. My tongue will praise You all the days of my life! In Jesus' name, Amen.

Now Sing!

What is your favorite song or hymn? Dear one, I encourage you to sing it. Now that you have been cleansed by His blood, it is time to sing!

Nehemiah 9:4–38 documents pure words of praise to the Lord. The Levites sang beautiful hymns and glorified

God. They praised who He was and what He had done. Let us now stop to recognize who God is and what He has done for us. Stop now and give Him praise.

Isaiah 54 is a chapter about singing. Verse one instructs the barren woman to sing over her womb. If you feel you have been unfruitful, then it is time to sing again. If Mammon has robbed you in any way, if you have allowed entrance to the enemy, if you have prepared him a room in your treasury, but now you have repented, then dear ones, it is time to sing!

7

Anointed to Defeat Mammon, Babylon and Divination

> As he neared Damascus on his journey, suddenly a light from heaven flashed around him. He fell to the ground and heard a voice say to him, "Saul, Saul, why do you persecute me?"
>
> Acts 9:3–4, NIV

Saul was legalistically bent on persecuting the Christians. This religious Jew set his face like flint toward Damascus to capture more prisoners who belonged to "The

Way." Little did he know that he was about to have a divine encounter with the One who was The Way!

"Thank goodness for the breezes that blow through this desolate place. I don't feel I could endure this heat without some relief." Saul sighed and reached once more for his water flask. Beads of sweat gathered upon his brow, and he searched for a cloth to wipe it.

Saul looked over his shoulder at the others who followed. "Anybody know how much longer it will be before we reach Damascus? I need a good meal and some rest!"

"Look ahead—see those hills?" one of his companions answered. "Just on the other side is Damascus. It is only a little farther." Saul heard the voice but was too exhausted and hot to turn his head to connect the voice with a person. Saul took a deep breath and forged ahead.

A camel would have been an easier ride, Saul thought. *At least I might have been able to sleep a bit while the camel plodded along.* His head began to nod as he attempted to steady himself on his horse. He began to imagine how he would present the letters from the high priest to the synagogues in Damascus, how he would arrest prisoners who followed The Way and take them back to the Jerusalem prisons. Hot, sweaty and exhausted, yet fueled with religious passion, he anticipated entering the city and fulfilling his commission.

Suddenly there was a flash of light! *What in the world?* Saul's mind raced ahead. *It cannot be lightning. There is no storm!* Then he fell to the ground.

A powerful voice—a voice that sounded like thunder and a mighty rushing river all at the same time—called out to him, "Saul." Then again, "Saul." The voice was speaking directly to him. "Why do you persecute me?" (Acts 9:4).

There was no doubt. Saul knew it was the voice of the Lord, but it was not the voice of Jehovah God that he had known all his life. "Who are you, Lord?" Saul asked (verse 5).

"I am Jesus, whom you are persecuting," the voice replied. "Now get up and go into the city, and you will be told what you must do" (verses 5–6).

Saul's mind felt as if lightning had struck it, as if an electrical charge had started there and then moved throughout his entire body. Talk about God dealing with a mindset! One minute Saul was pursuing Christians to imprison and later murder them for worshiping Jesus, and the next minute he was having an intimate encounter with the man he believed was an imposter and did not truly exist.

"Get up and go." The words of Jesus kept ringing in Saul's ears. *Get up? I can't move!* he thought. Not only that, but he also could not see; he had been completely blinded by the Light.

Those traveling with Saul were speechless, for they had seen the light but not heard the voice. Saul finally was able to get up from the ground and had to be led by the hand into the city of Damascus. He walked alongside the others, unable to ride his horse because of his blindness.

For three days Saul remained blind and was unable to eat or drink anything. Convicted and confused, he spent the time in intense prayer as he waited for instruction. *Lord, You said You would tell me what to do when I reached Damascus. I don't understand all of this. I recognize that You are Jesus. I ask for forgiveness for persecuting You and those who belong to The Way. Heal me, Lord Jesus. I beg You to return my sight and show me what I am to do for You. Please show me the way!*

As Saul prayed, the same heavenly voice spoke to a disciple of Christ who lived in Damascas: "Ananias!"

"Yes, Lord," Ananias answered immediately.

"Go to the house of Judas on Straight Street and ask for a man from Tarsus named Saul, for he is praying. In a vision he has seen a man named Ananias come and place his hands on him to restore his sight."

Ananias was taken back. "What? Lord, I have heard many reports about Saul from Tarsus—how he imprisons believers in Jerusalem and murders them. He has come here with authority from the high priest to arrest all of us who follow You." Ananias grew silent in the midst of his confusion. *Surely this cannot be the voice of God*, he thought to himself. His mind raced, and he envisioned his own death at the hands of Saul.

"Go!" the Lord commanded. "This man is my chosen instrument to carry my name before the Gentiles and their kings and before the people of Israel. I will show him how much he must suffer for my name" (Acts 9:15–16).

Ananias knew God meant business. *It is a good thing I know where Straight Street is*, he thought. Along the way Ananias reflected on the vision and the presence of the Lord, and as he did so he gained courage. Soon he spied the house. *Lord, help me!* The devout disciple forged ahead.

Soon he was standing before the man whose hands had led Christians to imprisonment and slaughter. Though he knew Saul could also imprison him, he forgot all animosity and laid his merciful hands, empowered and anointed by the Lord, upon Saul's blind eyes.

"Brother Saul, the Lord—Jesus, who appeared to you on the road as you were coming here—has sent me so that you may see again and be filled with the Holy Spirit" (verse 17).

Saul was amazed at Ananias's words and anointing. "Something is falling from my eyes!" Saul was almost jumping up and down. "As you prayed, something like scales fell from my eyes, and I can see again!"

Ananias, too, stood amazed. *To God be the glory*, he said to himself. *Lord, only You could do this!* For a brief moment, Ananias stood prepared to defend his life for fear that Saul might make an attempt to capture him. Yet at the same time the love of Christ consumed him for this man, Saul. *This man is truly called by You, Lord Jesus. I thank You for allowing me to be used for Your glory.*

After the supernatural healing, Saul arose and was immediately baptized. Soon he was able to eat again and regain his strength. He spent several days with the disciples in Damascus and then began to preach in the synagogues that Jesus Christ was the Son of God.

Saul's conversion was remarkable. Who else has ever had such a remarkable experience of meeting Christ—the blinding Light—on the way to imprison and kill believers? As he traveled the dusty highway, it probably never entered Saul's mind that on this road to Damascus he would be transformed into another person. He never imagined that here in the midst of the desert he would encounter the Lordship of Jesus Christ, the very One he persecuted. He could not have known that, yes, he did have a Kingdom destiny to fulfill, but instead of persecuting Christians he would be preaching and teaching the Kingdom message of Christ.

I believe that each of us has been on a Damascus road. We have experienced the power of the Light, the transformation of His Light and the call to be totally filled by His Spirit (see Acts 9:17). When we are filled with Him we have the power of God within us to overpower the spirits of darkness. The Greek word for *filled* in this passage is *pleroo*, which denotes being made full, or "to fill to the fullest." It also implies "to accomplish," or becoming completely full in God. It denotes a prophetic fulfillment, a divine overflowing, of all that God has planned for our personal destiny, a fullness that we then overflow onto others. In other words, God removed Saul's blindness and filled him with His Spirit so that the anointing would overflow onto others and others would believe in Christ, and He wants to do the same for us today. Wouldn't you love to become so full of God that His anointing oozed out from every pore and changed others?

Damascus

Saul's encounter with the one and only God could have been anywhere—Jerusalem, Rome, Ephesus. But he was on his way to Damascus. Why Damascus? Was this not just an ordinary road leading to a common city?

Damascus is a fertile plain, a circle thirty miles in diameter, that is surrounded by a desert that is completely desolate and infertile. Out of a narrow cleft in a nearby mountain the river Barada (called Abana in 2 Kings 5) gushes out life to the plain of Damascus lying beneath. Fruit of all kinds, especially olive trees, abound within this Damascus plain. So the waters emerge from a "narrow place" in the hillside down to a lush land of fruitfulness.

Saul, then, was on the road to Damascus. That is, he was probably in a wild desert setting looking for the narrow crossing into the lush, watered, fruitful plains. Well versed in Scripture and Jewish history, Saul understood the dynamics of the wilderness. His forefathers had crossed one themselves after they left Egypt for the Promised Land. He knew that in the midst of the wilderness Jehovah brought about transformation. It would not have escaped Saul that this desert experience on the road to Damascus was meant for his transformation. Similarly, the Lord often brings us through a wilderness experience to transform us and make us more like Christ in the end.

But perhaps the significance of Damascus lay in the fact that it was the most ancient city in Syria, the territory whose people worshiped Mammon as their principal god. And according to *Fausset's Bible Dictionary*, "Damascus was the center through which the trade of Tyre passed on its way to Assyria, Palmyra, Babylon and the East." It supplied "white wool and the wine of Helbon" (in Antilebanon, ten miles northwest of Damascus) in return for "the wares of Tyre's making" (see Ezekiel 27:18).[1] Damascus, then, was connected to the trade and merchandising of Tyre. Do you remember studying about the King of Tyre in chapter 3? You will recall that Tyre was connected to merchants and trade—Mammon and Babylon—and the King of Tyre was Satan personified. Indeed, God planned to use Saul (later called Paul) to expose the spirits attached to Mammon and Babylon.

Straight Street

Fausset's goes on to say that the street called "Straight" where Saul was healed from his blindness is actually still there![2] It would be hard not to notice the significance of the street name. Could it be that God was setting Saul straight? The Lord was making a straight path for Saul, empowering him for his future. Maybe He also was proving His faithfulness to Ananias and setting him straight. After all, a street named "Straight" would imply that it was the straight way, right?

Matthew 3:3 explains the Old Testament prophecy regarding the message of John the Baptist: "The voice of one crying in the wilderness (shouting in the desert), Prepare the road for the Lord, make His highways straight (level, direct)" (AMP).

Dear ones, we follow the same path today when we are seeking Him. Those of us who are blind to the truth may encounter the same blinding light, and scales will fall from our eyes. Do you desire this as much as I do? I want every hindrance, every evil mindset and blind spot to come into the Light and be exposed. I want God to set me straight! *Lord, as each believer reads this, remove the scales from his or her eyes so that each might truly see and be set straight by Your Spirit.*

Divination, Occult and Witchcraft Spirits

Paul (formerly Saul) traveled through many different territories and exposed several territorial demonic strongholds as he ministered the Gospel of the Kingdom. In my recent book, *Conquering the Antichrist Spirit*,[3] I exposed how Paul addressed the antichrist system in his travels. Now I will focus on how he was commissioned to address and expose the spirit of divination, the spirit of the occult and the spirit of witchcraft that pervaded Macedonia, and how these three are linked to Mammon and Babylon.

The Spirit of Divination

Acts 16:16 describes how Paul and Silas were on their way to prayer when a woman with a spirit of divination met them:

156

Once when we were going to the place of prayer, we were met by a slave girl who had a spirit by which she predicted the future. She earned a great deal of money for her owners by fortune-telling. This girl followed Paul and the rest of us, shouting, "These men are servants of the Most High God, who are telling you the way to be saved." She kept this up for many days. Finally Paul became so troubled that he turned around and said to the spirit, "In the name of Jesus Christ I command you to come out of her!" At that moment the spirit left her.

Acts 16:16–18

So Paul was on his way to prayer, and a girl who practiced witchcraft met them. Incidentally, it should not escape us that she was a slave girl, a young woman in bondage. Remember that if we submit to Mammon, it keeps us in bondage and enslaved in its demonic grip.

The Scripture states that the girl's counterfeit gifting of prophecy brought her employers much gain. In other words, she was employed by men who greatly profited from her fortune-telling. Talk about Mammon!

Why in the world would she go to meet with a man of God? Satan has no desire to be around the anointing of God, for fear of being cast out or exposed. Yet Satan sent her on a devilish assignment to distract the men of God and hinder their anointing. This is the assignment of Mammon and Babylon—to distract us from our mission in Christ.

As she followed Paul and Silas, the girl began to make a scene. She cried out, "These men are servants of the Most High God, who proclaim unto you the way of salvation" (ASV). On the surface it seemed the "religious" thing to say, for it sounded as if she were commending them for their gifting. But in reality she was causing a distraction and drawing attention to herself. She used false flattery to hide her motives. She was measuring her powers against God's, waiting for Paul and Silas to lose faith so that she could distract them and move in for the kill. She did this for many days, attempting to wear them down.

Some people would argue that Paul did not notice the disturbance. But I believe he was aware of it from the beginning. I believe he recognized something was wrong, but it may have taken him a while to discern what it was. He probably noticed confusion, experienced exhaustion and physical infirmity, lack of self-control and anger—all symptoms of divination. We do the same today. When divination opposes us and we know something does not seem right, we attempt to discern the spirit but doubt our discernment. Exhausted and mind-weary, maybe even ill, we question ourselves and walk around in total confusion.

So for several days the girl with the spirit of divination continued to bring attention to herself. Over the years in ministry my husband, Mickey, and I have encountered many of these types of spirits, which manifest as "religious" but actually draw attention to themselves. In some instances, for example, we have witnessed someone yelling so loudly that they completely distracted everyone else from worship. The entire focus of the gathering moved to the person acting religious—shaking, jerking or entering a trance-like state. It seemed at first that the person was giving God praise, but actually the spirit of divination was attempting to disguise itself as someone "religious." At other times, prophetic words have been declared so loudly and abruptly and at such the wrong time in the flow of worship that they bring only confusion. Again, this is the spirit of divination distracting God's people from His mission.

One must become discerning when dealing with such spirits. God does not compete with Himself. When these types of manifestations happen, I have learned to stop the voice of the enemy immediately and take control to allow the Spirit of God to move and minister. This is, after all, the example Paul set for us.

The Spirit of the Occult

The spirit of divination co-labors closely with the occult, and there is a fine line between the two. Remember that the spirit of divination distracts us from Christ's mission. The occult, then, attempts to hide revelation and understanding so that we cannot see the truth and therefore cannot become free. Jesus said that "the truth will make us free," and so the enemy works relentlessly to keep God's love and truth hidden from us. Any time areas remain hidden, the occult is at work.

After many days of listening to this spirit manifesting through the slave girl, Paul became "sore troubled," turned to the spirit of divination and said to it, " 'I charge thee in the name of Jesus Christ to come out of her.' And it came out that very hour" (Acts 16:18, ASV).

To be "sore troubled" means that he became grieved and anguished, which is easy to understand. The spirit of divination had opposed Paul for many days and was wearing him down. Then the spirit of the occult was hindering him from speaking truth. But further study reveals that this phrase meant he was troubled to the point of "starving" and had to "toil through" the demonic presence of the spirit of divination.[4] The spirit of the occult was so strong that Paul was in constant warfare and was starving for the presence of God! The demonic stronghold blocked Paul's spirit from being recharged by His presence on a daily basis.

159

Paul finally addressed that ugly spirit, and it came out in that very hour. Once he recognized the spirit for what it was, he turned toward the girl, addressed the spirit directly and commanded it to come out. Dear ones, you are empowered with the same Spirit Paul had, so do not hesitate: Rise up and speak with authority! *O Lord! I want the same to happen when I address that demonic stronghold!*

The Occult Mafia

A backlash, however, ensued. When the girl's employers (influenced by Mammon and the Babylonian system) saw that the spirit had left her and realized they could not make money off her any longer, they grew angry at Paul and Silas and dragged them into the marketplace before the magistrates. Sounds like the mafia to me! Like a scene out of *The Godfather*, the rulers of the marketplace rose up together against Paul and Silas, beat them and then tossed them into prison.

Believers, Mammon and the spirit of Babylon are rampant within our society today. Those who oppose the system are often charged on false pretenses for preaching the Gospel and praying against divination. I have known several ministers who actually were imprisoned as they attempted to shut down businesses of fortune-telling. We must stand firm together against these occult mafia strongholds and reclaim ground and wealth for God.

I used to drive by businesses that promoted fortune-telling and palm reading and claim the building/ground for the Kingdom of God. I have since learned to declare that the money gained there be given to the Kingdom of God. You see, it is really just all about the money (Mammon). Declaring the property to be used by God only empowers the spirit to find a new residence. If we claim the money to be used for the Gospel, however, then it really will shut down the entire enterprise.

We need to call for Kingdom money—money that is meant to spread the Gospel and not simply fill pocketbooks. If we have pure hearts when we pray against these occult businesses, then we will witness the same quick results that Paul did. Those spirits will leave within the hour—Hallelujah! When our hearts are pure, we will witness breakthroughs against Mammon and Babylon.

Breakthrough—but with Persecution

Most of us know the rest of the story. Paul and Silas were beaten and imprisoned in the inner prison, their feet fastened into stocks:

And at midnight Paul and Silas prayed, and sang praises unto God: and the prisoners heard them. And suddenly there was a great earthquake, so that the foundations of the prison were shaken: and immediately all the doors were opened, and every one's bands were loosed. And the keeper of the prison awaking out of his sleep, and seeing the prison doors open, he drew out his sword, and would have killed himself, supposing that the prisoners had been fled. But Paul cried with a loud voice, saying, Do thyself no harm: for we are all here. Then he called for a light, and sprang in, and came trembling, and fell down before Paul and Silas, and brought them out, and said, Sirs, what must I do to be saved? And they said, Believe on the Lord Jesus Christ, and thou shalt be saved, and thy house. And they spake unto him the word of the Lord, and to all that were in his house. And he took them the same hour of the night, and washed their stripes; and was baptized, he and all his, straightway. And when he had brought them into his house, he set meat before them, and rejoiced, believing in God with all his house. And when it was day, the magistrates sent the serjeants, saying, Let those men go.

Acts 16:25–35, KJV

Dear ones, a person serving God as a Kingdom minister, who desires to use Kingdom wealth to build God's Kingdom, will suffer persecution. No doubt about it. I am a living testimony. Each new chapter I write opens more opportunities for Mammon to strike at me. I cannot begin to tell you how many times money has been an issue since beginning to write this book. Yet I remain committed to expose this demonic force of darkness. Like Paul, who even at the risk of imprisonment addressed the evil behind Mammon and Babylon and stood up to the spirits of lust, greed and perversion, I am setting my face like flint to finish this race. Will you join me?

If we persevere and boldly address the occult spirits of Mammon and Babylon, think of what can happen. Just as they did for Paul and Silas, angels will shake the demonic structures that attempt to imprison us. We will experience a supernatural earthquake, the prison doors will open wide, our bonds will be loosed from us and many will become saved.

Symptoms of an Occult Stronghold

Has your money supply been cut off? Most of us are feeling the economic crunch, but is there more to it? Have you allowed room for a spirit of divination? Let me explain further how this spirit operates and then you will know for certain if you have given the occult a seated position in your finances.

1. *Sleeping with the Enemy—Divination!*

The word *divination* is linked to the Greek word *puthon*, which is closely connected to the name *python*. *Putho* was the name of the region where Delphi, the seat of the famous oracle, was located, which was where a soothsayer, or diviner, was inspired to prophesy falsely.[5]

A python, of course, squeezes the breath from its victims and suffocates them. Believers, the enemy is after the breath of Life that we take to others. When the slave girl employed by Babylon sought out Paul and Silas, she sought to suffocate the breath of Life they brought to others as they preached the Gospel. Christians in the marketplace struggle against a python spirit because they are givers and tithers who promote the Kingdom of God. The enemy does not want believers to minister the Gospel, therefore he attempts to suffocate us—cut off our lifeline and squeeze the life out of our vision.

My sister told me a story of a young girl who had an actual python as a pet! Yes, I know—a pet. The girl actually slept with her python at night. Over time she began to notice that her pet snake quit eating. After a few weeks, she and her mother contacted a local veterinarian. The vet told them that a python quits eating as it gets near to its victim because it begins to measure its length against its victim. In other words, it is thinking, *How long must I get before I am able to grab the head of my victim and then wrap the rest of my body around it to squeeze the life from it?* Believers, this snake was measuring its length at night as it slept beside its owner, and it quit eating because it was awaiting its opportunity to bite her head, squeeze out her life and consume her! This girl really was "sleeping with the enemy." Dear ones, be careful what you become familiar with.

163

We must wake up—literally and figuratively. We can tolerate divination no more. We must allow God to expose it by letting go of our past, our control and concerns for our future. We must fully trust God and not Mammon. We must not come into agreement with Babylon, but instead use discernment and money to build God's Kingdom, not our own. We must trust God and ask God how He desires for us to move forward. Uncertain times should propel us toward God rather than cause us to flee in fear from His presence. If you find yourself running away from God, then repent and return to Him.

2. *Tolerating Jezebel*

I have written much on Jezebel over the years, but it is important here to focus on Jezebel as she relates to Mammon. The demonic spirit of Jezebel uses false flattery to control us concerning money issues. When money is involved, Jezebel attempts to quickly seduce us with false flattery. Has someone ever said wonderful things about you to make you feel you could trust him, and then followed the false flattery with a question: "Can I borrow some money?" We cannot let counterfeit flattery go to our heads and get puffed up with pride. All of us like to hear good things about ourselves, but we must not tolerate Jezebel and her false flattery. Anyone who attempts to control you with manipulation, desiring money or gain, is being controlled by the spirits of Jezebel, divination and Mammon. Rebuke them and command them to go!

3. *Not Discerning Truth*

In Exodus 7:9–12, Pharaoh called for his wise men, who were skilled in magic and divination, and they performed a "copycat" of many of Moses' miracles. Similarly today,

164

we are bombarded with people, ads and television shows that promote divination, counterfeit anointing and false signs and wonders. They ask for donations and monthly financial support. They present "needs" that are not godly needs. We must be aware of spiritual seduction concerning our giving. Dear believers, we need a heightened level of discernment for these end times.

Webster's Dictionary defines *discernment* as "to see or understand the difference, to make a distinction; as to discern between good and evil, truth and falsehood."[6] This definition reminds me once again of Saul, who could not see the truth and so murdered those who were of the truth. Only a blinding light released true sight. Encountering Jesus on the road to Damascus enabled Saul to discern the truth. And by encountering the Truth, he was equipped also to discern false truth—the spirits of divination, the occult and witchcraft.

Discernment takes practice. Be on guard, so that you are not deceived. Keep your spirit in tune with the right "sound" from heaven! Do not listen to false sounds, for they are the voice of the enemy.

4. *Money-Motivated Ministry*

As children of God, we all are ordained by God to minister. One does not need a pulpit to "pull people from the pit"; each of us is a minister right where we are. We can lead unbelievers to Christ in the grocery store, in the parking lot or wherever the Lord directs.

Those of us, however, who serve in full-time ministry are at increased risk for being seduced by the spirit of Mammon, and we can never allow Mammon to defile our motives when we minister the Gospel. Though I travel and receive love offerings whenever I minister, I cannot allow my ministry to be controlled by large offerings. I know ministers who have become hirelings, traveling and ministering only because they are money-motivated. We must be careful about such a serious matter. Micah 3:11–12 paints a vivid picture of prophets who prophesy for money, leaders who accept bribes and teachers who teach only for a price. God says that disaster will surely come to them, for "Zion will be plowed like a field" because the Church has allowed Mammon to seduce them.

Barnes' Notes links this passage directly with divination, connecting these prophets with "false prophecy" and those who "divine" for money.[7] This is the same spirit that controlled the slave girl as she labored for her employers. The passage refers to one "judging for rewards," as if he expects some type of payback for his judgment. Dear believers, paybacks in spiritual politics are not of the Lord. Ministering, judging darkness and teaching the Gospel should be out of obedience rather than out of a motivation for money. We are to seek first the Kingdom and teach for the glory of God. We should regard temporal and earthly rewards as secondary.

Believers, nothing is more detestable to me than a prophet who is motivated and swayed by money. Sadly, over the years I have witnessed many who prophesy to others, telling them how much money to give them as a minister. This grieves me. Jesus never did this, and neither should any of us. We must realize the demonic seductions of the ministers of the Gospel who become deceived in their gifting and manipulate others to give financially to their ministries.

Remember Balaam? Balak asked him to curse Israel. If he did so Balak promised to give him a large sum of money. Balaam would not directly curse Israel, but motivated by Mammon he eventually found a way for Israel to become cursed without prophesying over it. He encouraged Israel to intermarry, knowing it would displease God and bring a curse upon the entire nation. Thus, he got paid for his counsel. Because of his evil seduction, the New Testament refers to Balaam as a false prophet. When spiritual leaders are motivated by money, it is Mammon—plain and simple.

I have tried to witness the Gospel, on the other hand, to many who tout the ancient excuse, "All the church wants from me is my money." To a degree, I understand their feelings. None of us, however, should allow this to become an excuse for not submitting to God and giving our tithes. The tithe already belongs to God; we simply need to know where to give it.

Do not allow manipulation and control to hoodwink you. If someone is in need, do not act out of a knee-jerk reaction of mercy. Take time, pray and give accordingly. In other words, do not give place to Mammon, or else you become a slave.

You Can't Take It with You

How long will we tolerate Mammon and Babylon? How long are we to remain in the wilderness? Will it take God knocking us from a prideful, religiously bent position to awaken us? Are we truly blinded to the principles of Christ and "The Way"?

I know I had to be taken down a few notches. During our recent move to our ranch I found myself with little storage space. As I mentioned earlier, I had to decide what I could hold onto and what I was willing to let go. I recall looking over a sea of unpacked boxes and feeling anger and resentment, then yelling out in frustration, "Heavenly days, what am I to do with all this stuff?"

As I have described to you, I had no room for many of our things—even items that had cost us a lot of money—and had to give them to Goodwill. I remember stopping in front of a drop-off site and letting go of my valuables. I drove off sadly, ashamed of my pride. Had I allowed Tobiah a room in my treasury? I believe I had. My heart was unclean, and I valued my stuff more than I valued the blessing of blessing others with it. My "things" had taken up space in my heart and had become my treasure. Believers, nothing—no amount of money, no relationship, no one thing—should ever block our relationship with Christ. If things are a hindrance, then get them out! Cleanse your temple and cast darkness out of your living quarters and heart.

We cannot take one single thing with us to heaven. When my father died, he left this earth with nothing. The Lord had blessed him in his earthly life, and his dead body still bore his rings with sparkling diamonds and his money clip filled with cash. I distinctly remember looking around at all the things he had accumulated during his lifetime and realizing that nothing goes with us to heaven except our souls.

So, precious ones, it is time to surrender. All that we possess is God's. We will find total freedom if today, right now—this very second—we will give Him all of us.

This is a really good opportunity to spend some private time with the Lord. Start by reading 1 Corinthians 13:13. Realize that when all things are passed away, only three things remain—faith, hope and love. Ask Him to empower you to prioritize the things that will remain.

List below what you need to surrender completely to Him:

1. _____

2. _____

3. _____

4. _____

5. _____

Now ask Him in your own words—from the bottom of your heart—to empower you with a new level of faith to trust Him, to give you a new hope for your future and to allow you to know His love so that you can shift into all that He has for your future.

8

It Is Written!

Jesus said to him, "Away from me, Satan!
For it is written: 'Worship the Lord your
God, and serve him only.'"

Matthew 4:10, NIV

As I continue to write on the spirits of Mammon and Babylon, I find myself more deeply in love with my Savior. The depths of His love draw me into deeper revelation and understanding. This book is the result of my seeking an even greater level of freedom in Christ and intimacy with Him. Like David, my soul longs to know Him more. Psalm 42:1–2 describes my heart (and hopefully yours): "As the deer pants for streams of water, so my soul pants for you, O God. My soul thirsts for God, for the living God." I pray you will allow Him to touch the depths of your heart, too, as you continue to read.

Yet in my struggles I have cried many tears and have even wondered, *Does God really care?* In uncertain times I have felt as if my soul was cast down. The original word for "cast down" is *shachach,* meaning to sink or depress. It is connected to the words *bend* or *bow down.* This implies a "bowing down" to idolatry.

To bow down to something is a way of paying homage—actually "serving." Remember that we cannot serve two masters. We will serve either God or Mammon. As children of God, we must ensure that we are bowing down only to Him, and Him alone. Satan will challenge us, tempting us to bow to him, and we need to know how to resist his evil schemes. Our Savior Himself gives us the best example.

While in the wilderness before beginning His formal ministry, Jesus was tested by Satan, who tempted Jesus to bow down and serve him. And Satan used the demonic forces of Mammon and the Babylonian system in his evil temptation of our Lord. I am going to turn now to the story of Jesus' temptation. As you read, please remember that God often allows the spaces between biblical sentences to captivate our imaginations, ponder His truths and allow His Word to plow our hearts.

Jesus Defeated Satan in the Wilderness

It was the Spirit of God who led Jesus into the desert to be tempted by Satan. Imagine yourself in Jesus' shoes for a moment. You would have been fasting for forty days and forty nights, severely weak and hungry. The tempter, knowing your state, comes to you and tempts you with the one thing your body is craving most: "If you are truly the Son of God, then turn these stones into bread" (see Matthew 4:1–4). Mountains of stone are all around you. How easy it would be for you to make bread!

Satan tempted Jesus with provision. Do you see the connection to Mammon? Satan used the spirit of Mammon to tempt Jesus to look to him as the provider, rather than God. If Jesus had bowed down to Satan's evil temptation, then He would have served Mammon and entered into bondage.

Jesus, however, knew who His Provider was. He knew that if the Spirit of God had led Him into the wilderness, then the Spirit would also strengthen Him in that desert without His having to bow down to His enemy, and He knew the Spirit would provide for all His needs.

Remember how Jesus taught His disciples to pray? "Give us this day our daily bread." By "bread" He did not simply mean food; "bread" also implied "provision." In the same way he tempted Jesus in the wilderness, Mammon tempts us today not to trust our Father for provision.

The devil does not have any new ideas. He just uses the same temptations over and over again. Look at Eve in the Garden; Satan tempted her, too, with food. He tempts us when we are hungry, dry, thirsty, alone or feeling abandoned—in a "desert" experience. He comes when our appetites are fierce, and when we are in such a place it is easy to fight temptation with our souls rather than by the Holy Spirit.

How did Jesus fight the temptation of the devil? Studying His response gives us the tools we need to fight by the Spirit.

Jesus responded, "*It is written*: 'Man does not live on bread alone, but on every word that comes from the mouth of God'" (Matthew 4:4, emphasis added). Do you see what He did? Jesus quoted God's Holy Word to resist temptation and set the ground rules for His Lordship. He knew this wilderness temptation was necessary before He could leave the desert in victory and move forward into His authority with signs, wonders and miracles. He merely spoke the Word of God, which defeated Mammon and its false provision.

Satan did not give up easily, and he moved on to the next temptation. He took Jesus to the holy city and had Jesus stand on the highest point of the Temple. Satan said to Him.

> If you are the Son of God, . . . throw yourself down. For *it is written*: "He will command his angels concerning you, and they will lift you up in their hands, so that you will not strike your foot against a stone."
>
> Matthew 4:6, emphasis added

Let's be clear about what Satan did. Jesus had used God's Word to resist His enemy the first time. Satan slyly picked up on that and then used the Word to try to seduce the Living Word. How twisted is that? He used the Word against the Word.

Furthermore, what would have happened if Jesus had given in to Satan's temptation? Satan's leading Jesus to the Temple mount suggests that he hoped for some dramatic scene where Jesus would jump and angels would save Him. All the Jews below would have then recognized Christ before He faced the cross. If Jesus had surrendered to this plan and foregone the shedding of His blood, then while He would still be God He would not have been able to save any of us, and we would be lost.

Jesus, however, wisely recognized Satan's seduction and his desire to obscure the truth. He responded again with the Word of God, by which every temptation is overcome: "Jesus answered him, '*It is also written*: "Do not put the Lord your God to the test"'" (verse 7, emphasis added).

Have you ever put God to a test? I know I have. When I do what I know I should not, then I am testing His love for me. And I often fail Satan's tests. When Mammon, for example, raises its ugly head and I fall into its trap, fretting over money, then I am failing another test. Whenever I face the Babylonian system and focus on the stock market and investment portfolios rather than trust in God's ability to provide for my future, then I am failing once more. I have failed all too often. When will I learn to trust Him completely for my provision? Does He not promise to clothe me, to provide for me? Often in the hour of temptation I am weak. Yet I am so thankful that in His hour of temptation Jesus was strong and decided not to test God. *Thank You, Lord, for Your everlasting love and that You passed the test for me!*

The third temptation of Christ has always amazed me. Satan took Jesus to a high mountain and showed Him all the kingdoms of the world and their splendor. "'All this I will give you,' he said, 'if you will bow down and worship me'" (verse 9). How could Satan ever believe that Jesus would actually bow down and worship him? To do so would be to bow down to everything dark and evil.

Jesus looked beyond that brief moment and saw the future. To yield His authority would empower Satan as CEO over all the kingdoms of the world. It would have put every kingdom for all time—all of us!—completely under the influence of the Babylonian system. Imagine each of us having to bow down daily to an antichrist structure. If Jesus had bowed, then He would have surrendered His authority—but also He would have surrendered *our* authority in Christ. In other words, we would have no authority in the name of Jesus to defeat our enemy! Jesus knew that if He bowed to Satan, then the world would be filled with oppression, poverty, violence and everything evil with no hope of salvation. Furthermore, Jesus knew that "all this" was not Satan's to give, for it belonged to the Creator God.

Once more Jesus used Scripture to defeat His enemy:

Jesus said to him, "Away from me, Satan! For *it is written*: 'Worship the Lord your God, and serve him only.'" Then the devil left him, and angels came and attended him.

verses 10–11, emphasis added

Again, we cannot serve two masters. We must serve either God or Mammon. I know I am hammering this in, but I believe each revelation needs adequate attention so that we can properly apply it to our lives. Christ's experience in the desert proved that He lived by the very same requirements of faith and ultimate dependence on the Father by which each of us must live. As we build God's Kingdom on the earth, Satan will use the spirit of Mammon to sow doubt in our hearts concerning God's faithfulness in the same way that he did with Jesus in the wilderness. We must always trust God and Him only during uncertain times.

And, dear ones, we must always remind ourselves that our strength lies in our ability to speak His Word to the enemy. "It is written!"

Becoming a Light in the Darkness

After His temptation, Jesus came out of the wilderness endued with authority and great power. Luke 4:14 states, "Jesus returned in the power of the Spirit into Galilee: and there went out a fame of him through all the region round about" (KJV). The Greek word for *power* is *dunamis*, from which we get our English word *dynamite*. *Dunamis*, then, describes a miraculous "dynamite" power—an exploding power to do mighty works and miracles. It also refers to physical strength. One can say, therefore, that God also gives us strength (*dunamis*) to overcome the enemy at the time of temptation.

Scripture tells us that after Jesus' temptation, the devil left Him and God sent angels to minister to Him. Then He heard that John the Baptist had been imprisoned, and He returned to Galilee. Leaving Nazareth, He went to live in Capernaum—all fulfilling what was said through the prophet Isaiah:

> Land of Zebulun and land of Naphtali, the way to the sea, along the Jordan, Galilee of the Gentiles—the people living in darkness have seen a great light; on those living in the land of the shadow of death a light has dawned.
>
> Matthew 4:15–16

Jesus overcame temptation knowing that He had a future—to become a "great light" in the midst of "people living in darkness," in "the land of the shadow of death." From that time on Jesus began to preach, "Repent, for the kingdom of heaven is near"(verse 17).

And His light drew His followers. As He walked beside the Sea of Galilee, He saw two brothers, Simon called

Peter and his brother Andrew. As they cast their fishing nets into the lake, Jesus called out to them, "Come, follow me . . . and I will make you fishers of men" (verse 19). At once—literally in an instant—they left those nets and followed Him. Jesus later saw two other brothers, James and John. Jesus called out to them and they also "immediately . . . left the boat and their father and followed him" (verse 22). I have always been amazed at the quick decision of these men to leave everything behind and follow Jesus. His "light" must have been so bright, and He must have spoken with such *dunamis* and authority that it left no question in their minds.

Can we become great lights, too? Can we walk in the same authority as Christ? Don't we have something inside us that draws others? If we have received Jesus as our Savior and are following Him, then we are lights in the midst of darkness. We have been given the same power to overcome the kingdoms of this world.

> And Jesus went about all Galilee, teaching in their synagogues, and preaching the gospel of the kingdom, and healing all manner of sickness and all manner of disease among the people. And his fame went throughout all Syria: and they brought unto him all sick people that were taken with divers diseases and torments, and those which were possessed with devils, and those which were lunatick, and those that had the palsy; and he healed them. And there followed him great multitudes of people from Galilee, and from Decapolis, and from Jerusalem, and from Judea, and from beyond Jordan.
>
> Matthew 4:23–25, KJV

Jesus' power was truly wonder-working. Overcoming the temptations of Satan in the wilderness empowered

Him to move out in *dunamis* to bring light and healing to a broken world. That same authority and power, dear ones, is available to us today.

Our Savior defeated Satan in the wilderness because He purposed our freedom. It is our destiny to be free indeed. Knowing He had a Kingdom message to preach, a people to prepare and enemies to defeat, Jesus set His face as flint toward the cross. He had much to do in His ministry of three years, so He moved purposely and in His Father's timing.

Confronting Mammon

After His time in the wilderness, Jesus was fueled with a passion to serve the Father. He was jealous over His Father's name and reputation and desired to show honor to His house. He therefore boldly confronted Mammon and the Babylonian money system at the Temple.

The Temple of God had attracted money changers, those who exchanged foreign money for a profit. They had set up their lucrative businesses in the courts of God. This was Mammon, pure and simple, boldly overstepping a boundary of holiness with an "in-your-face" attitude toward the Father.

In their insightful book *Elijah's Revolution*, James W. Goll and Lou Engle write about Jesus driving out the money changers:

> The money changers and dove sellers were running an officially sanctioned operation of graft, greed and dishonesty. They cheated people by charging exorbitant prices to exchange standard currency into Temple currency that was acceptable for offerings, and to provide "pre-approved" animals for sacrifice to replace those that they found, often

without just cause, blemished or otherwise unacceptable. By approving of this arrangement, from which they received "kickbacks," the priests and other religious leaders, those who were entrusted with representing God before the people, dishonored God's house and sullied His reputation.[1]

Could that sound any more like Mammon and the perverted Babylonian system? Satan was not simply in the wilderness—he was in the place of sacrifice and worship! Money, greed, covetousness and every evil spirit attached to it was in God's house.

Jesus discerned immediately the evil that had to be driven out of the Temple of God. To confront Mammon and the filthy Babylonian system in the Temple, Jesus used the same words He had used to defeat Satan in the wilderness: "*It is written*" he said to them, 'My house will be called a house of prayer,' but you are making it a 'den of robbers' " (Matthew 21:13, emphasis added).

"It is written." This is a key for us today. We must use God's Word to destroy the ungodly structures that block our breakthroughs.

Deluded and Blinded

When He confronted the money changers, Jesus proclaimed that His house would not be a den of robbers—those who serve Mammon rather than God. Would He find the same in the house of our hearts? Is Mammon in our temple? Do we serve Mammon in our hearts rather than God?

I have to admit that I have probably spent more time during the writing of this book fretting over provision and cares of this world than I have going to God in prayer. My house has been one of worry, frustration and concern rather than prayer. I have been deluded. Scripture tells us that our old nature is corrupted with delusion, and we have to be removed from that old nature and renewed in our minds in order to be transformed into God's image:

> Strip yourselves of your former nature [put off and discard your old unrenewed self] which characterized your previous manner of life and becomes corrupt through lusts and desires that spring from *delusion*; and be constantly *renewed in the spirit* of your mind [having a fresh mental and spiritual attitude], and put on the new nature (the regenerate self) created in God's image, [Godlike] in true righteousness and holiness.
>
> Ephesians 4:22–24, AMP, emphasis added

The word *delusion* means "something that is falsely or delusively believed or propagated, a persistent, false, psychotic belief regarding the self or persons or objects, and (also) the abnormal state marked by such beliefs. Synonyms describing delusion or being deluded are: illusion, hallucination and a mirage—all meaning something believed to be true and real but that is actually false or unreal, often as the result of a disordered state of mind."[2]

Delusion is strongly linked to witchcraft and the occult. One might say that Satan speaks his lies and casts his spell, mesmerizing us to believe them. Since Mammon and the Babylonian system have an idolatrous root, witchcraft and delusion work alongside them to actively oppress us. When we are deluded, we are blinded to the truth.

Second Corinthians 4:4 says, "The god of this age has blinded the minds of unbelievers, so that they cannot see the light of the gospel of the glory of Christ, who is the image of God." The original word for *blind* here is *tuphlos.* It means "to envelop with smoke, to be unable to see clearly." In other words, the enemy puts up a smoke screen and blinds us to the truth. And Satan's blinding us to the truth is a clear manifestation of an occult spirit because the occult attempts to keep things hidden. It deludes us.

Second Thessalonians 2:8–12 reveals that in the end times the lawless one (the Antichrist and the antichrist system) will be revealed, and delusion will be active. Satan will display counterfeit miracles, signs and wonders. This passage even says that because people love evil over truth, God will send them a powerful delusion, and they will believe the lies of their enemy. In other words, if we agree with Satan, then God will allow us to become deluded and believe a lie. How frightening is that? I certainly do not want to be turned over to a reprobate mind or suffer delusion, do you?

When we embrace an antichrist system, we also are agreeing with evil. Dear ones, we must be careful not to agree with the enemy. We cannot serve both God and Mammon. We must make a choice.

In uncertain times, such as when we face a financial crisis, the enemy attempts to seduce us with lies regarding our provision. During such fiery trials our "certainty" becomes challenged as the devil tries to cloud our vision. Not to trust God is also to believe that He is not able to provide for us. To need certainty about our future is to open the door to the occult and the spirit of witchcraft.

We need spiritual eyes to see the truth. Simple trust in God and speaking His Word will cause the devil to flee. God expects us to trust Him. He desires that we be like Abraham, who stepped forth in total faith. Let us not be deluded or blinded but walk in complete faith in our Provider.

Mammon and the Seven Deadly Sins

When I was a child I made the transition one Sunday from Sunday school class, where simple Bible stories are taught, to "adult church." I enjoyed singing my favorite hymns, but the pastor's message that day on the seven deadly sins went right over my head. Yet somehow his message affected me enough that I became concerned I needed "fire insurance." Understanding that I needed Jesus as my Savior, I ran down the aisle as fast as my short legs would carry me. I did not learn much about the deadly sins again until I did some extended research on Mammon. And to my surprise—and I really do mean it was a surprise—Mammon (the love of money and the greed attached to it) is considered a "deadly sin."

Some sins actually build what I describe as a "death structure," and this is why these sins are called the seven "deadly" sins. A death structure is when the enemy comes in with a temptation or seduction. When we agree with his lies, he is then committed to a takeover: He begins to build "his house" within our hearts and lives. Satan looks for every opportunity to destroy us, kill us and steal our futures.

According to Wikipedia, the seven deadly sins also have been known as the "capital vices or cardinal sins," and are a classification of the "most objectionable vices that have been used since early Christian times to educate and instruct followers concerning (immoral) fallen man's tendency to sin. They are: lust, gluttony, greed, sloth, wrath, envy and pride."[3]

The seven deadly sins are included in Galatians 5:19–21. Though this passage lists many more than seven sins, there is consensus among theologians that they all fit into a category of seven:

The acts of the sinful nature are obvious: sexual immorality, impurity and debauchery; idolatry and witchcraft; hatred, discord, jealousy, fits of rage, selfish ambition, dissensions, factions and envy; drunkenness, orgies, and the like. I warn you, as I did before, that those who live like this will not inherit the kingdom of God.

Let's take a closer look at the seven sins that are considered *deadly*:

- *Lust* (fornication)—unlawful sexual desire, such as desiring sex with a person outside of marriage.
- *Gluttony*—wastefulness, whether it is consuming too much food, drink or drugs; misplaced desire; not giving to the needy.
- *Greed* (covetousness, avarice)—desiring more things than one needs or can use. Dante wrote that greed is too much "love of money and power." (This is Mammon!)
- *Sloth*—laziness, idleness and wastefulness of time.
- *Wrath* (anger, hate)—inappropriate (wrong) feelings of hatred, revenge or even denial, as well as punitive desires outside of justice. This would include being spiteful and desiring revenge.
- *Envy* (jealousy)—hating other people for what they have.
- *Pride* (vanity)—a desire to be important or attractive to others or excessive love of self.

Wikipedia also lists extravagance (in Latin, *luxuria*—where we derive our word *luxury*) as a deadly sin. Extravagance is "unrestrained excess." It includes the frequent purchase of luxury goods and forms of debauchery and involves the love of money. Once again, the connection to Mammon and the Babylonian system of wealth is obvious.

While greed is clearly motivated by Mammon, other deadly sins are as well. Gluttony, which in essence is not trusting God to be one's Provider and hoarding instead, is motivated by Mammon, as is envy, which involves desiring another's goods and is connected to covetousness and chronic dissatisfaction.

To counteract the seven deadly sins we must again look to God's Word, for everything we need to tear down the death structures of Satan "is written." We need, for example, to focus on the fruit of the Spirit and ask God to develop it in our lives:

> But the fruit of the Spirit is love, joy, peace, patience, kindness, goodness, faithfulness, gentleness, self-control; against such things there is no law. Now those who belong to Christ Jesus have crucified the flesh with its passions and desires. If we live by the Spirit, let us also walk by the Spirit. Let us not become boastful, challenging one another, envying one another.
>
> Galatians 5:22–26, NASB

Here in God's Word we find the tools we need to counteract the seven deadly sins. By fostering His Word and His truths in our hearts, we are given the *dunamis* we need to battle our enemy.

But we must first be aware of the wiles of the enemy. If we are not, then we will never experience victory. Satan does *not* desire that we recognize his schemes. We must renounce all wickedness and sinful desires if we are to become free of Mammon.

The book of Proverbs states that God specifically hates six things, "and the seventh His soul detests" (see Proverbs 6:16–19):

1. Haughty eyes
2. A lying tongue
3. Hands that shed innocent blood
4. A heart that devises wicked plots
5. Feet that are swift to run into mischief
6. A deceitful witness that utters lies
7. He that sows discord among brethren

Though this is a somewhat different list from the list in Galatians, God is obviously quite concerned about sin. When we are tempted to fall into sin, the enemy is attempting to seduce us with his lies. We cannot let his deception cloud our vision and persuade us not to trust God. Remember that Jesus is our example in overcoming sin. The way to overcome the death structures of the seven deadly sins is by the Word of God.

"It is written."

The Sin of Unbelief

Remember that Mammon tries to seduce us with lies regarding our provision. When we are tempted not to trust God in any way, we are committing the sin of unbelief. In other words, we are not believing that God is able to provide for all our needs, and this is sin.

Jesus hated the sin of unbelief. Look at what He said:

> "O unbelieving generation," Jesus replied, "how long shall I stay with you? How long shall I put up with you?"
>
> Mark 9:19

To think that Jesus ever feels that He has to "put up" with me grieves me! Yet when my faith level is low, He has to do just that.

After studying the meaning of the word *unbelief*, I better understand Jesus' response. It means "not worthy of confidence and (being) untrustworthy." In other words, when we do not believe in His provision we do not have confidence in Him, and we consider Him to be untrustworthy. It is like Jesus is saying in this passage, "Why don't you trust Me to heal you? Don't you trust Me to provide for you? How long do I have to put up with your listening to the enemy who convinces you that I am untrustworthy?"

Have we believed the lie that God is untrustworthy? Do we spend more time agonizing than we do praying and worshiping? Our Lord is able in every way to do exceeding above what we could ever think or imagine. So why do we consider Him untrustworthy? We are committing a sin: the sin of unbelief.

The way to overcome spiritual blindness is to begin to "see" again. We can always look to God's Word to help us see rightly. After all, "It is written."

As the sin of unbelief questions the character of God—who He is—let us look, then, to His Word to see what He says about Himself. God uses a number of names in the Old Testament for Himself. Each speaks to a different aspect of His character. He calls Himself:

Elohim—The Creator (the One Who Created Us)
El Elyon—The God Most High (God Almighty)
Adonai—Sovereign Lord (Our Lord and Master)
Jehovah—The Self-Existent God
Jehovah Jireh—God Our Provider

Jehovah Shalom—God of Peace

Jehovah Nissi—God Who Is Our Banner of Victory

Jehovah Tsidkenu—God Our Righteousness

El Shaddai—The All-Sufficient One

El Roi—The God Who Sees

Jehovah Raah—The Lord Our Shepherd

Jehovah Mekoddishkem—God Who Is Our Sanctification

Jehovah Shammah—The Lord Is Present with Us

Jehovah Baal Perez—The Lord of Breakthrough

Jehovah Sabaoth—The Lord of Hosts

Jehovah Rapha—The Lord Our Healer/Physician

Abba Father—Our Lover and Protector ("Daddy" Who Loves Us)

Dear ones, it is time to stop agonizing about your situation and start developing a deeper prayer life. By concentrating on who God is, you will gain victory over your enemy. When you pray, focus on what He says in His Word, on the names He calls Himself. By doing so you will be empowered to believe for breakthrough and to cycle out of an old, unbelieving, destructive pattern. When you are faced with financial challenges, for example, speak to your enemy that God is your Jehovah Jireh, your Provider. When you begin to worry from where your provision will come, state that He is your El Shaddai, your All-Sufficient One. Speak to your enemy, dear ones. Tell him, "It is written!"

Which name do you have difficulty embracing? Do you truly believe that God is your Jehovah Jireh? Do you know in your heart that He is Jehovah Rapha? Do you believe He really is your El Roi who sees your pain, and your

Jehovah Shammah, who is present with you in it? Do you need Him to step in on your behalf and be your Jehovah Sabaoth? Do you believe He is your Jehovah Nissi, who will give you the victory?

This is an important moment in your history. Spend time with Him today. Embrace who He says He is and come into agreement with Him, believing that He is the God who does not lie. He is dependable, and He is trustworthy. He is your Alpha and Omega, and He has your future in His hands. Will you believe today? You can. After all, "It is written."

A Prayer of Repentance

Allow me to lead you in a prayer of repentance to break the death structures off of you and your generations.

Father, in the name of Jesus, I repent for my involvement in any of the deadly sins. I repent for allowing Mammon and the spirit of Babylon to influence my decisions concerning money and my finances. I repent especially for the sins that I am aware of, such as (name them as God shows them to you). I renounce any involvement with demonic activity and the occult. I command the demons attached to my sins to flee and be removed from my life in the name of Jesus. I repent for the sin of not trusting You for provision. I declare to the devil, "It is written" that I will not live by bread alone, but by every word that comes from the mouth of God. I also say, "It is written" (now is the time to address your unbelief concerning God and His Word . . . quote specific biblical passages that address your needs and tell the devil what God says about you and your generations. You also may include the specific names of God that pertain to your situation.)

189

I not only repent of my sins, but I also repent for the sins of my generations and ask for Your divine forgiveness. I plead the blood of Jesus over myself and my generations. Lord, I thank You for forgiving me and for giving me abundant life in the name of Jesus Christ. Amen.

Now, dear ones:

B elieve that He is who He says He is: the great I AM.

E very word that is written is His covenant promise for you.

L ive every day believing that He will watch over His words and perform them.

I nvite Him into every area of your life and trust Him to take care of you.

E very time the enemy attempts to seduce you, say, "Devil, it is written!"

V ictory begins with what you say with your mouth and believe in your heart.

E ach time you are tempted to doubt God, remember who He says He is.

9

Too Close to Home

Now Naaman, captain of the host of the
king of Syria, was a great man with his
master, and honourable, because by him
the LORD had given deliverance unto Syria:
he was also a mighty man in valour, but
he was a leper.

2 Kings 5:1, KJV

Look at him! Look at the *great* commander now!" The
foot soldier snickered and pointed toward Naaman,
the commander of the Syrian forces.

"Yeah! He stood tall on the battlefield, but look at him today—plagued with leprosy. I cannot bear to look upon him. How disgusting! No one will be able to look at him and serve under him now. In my opinion, he has thought so highly of himself for so long—well, he deserves to come down a few notches." Both soldiers were consumed with bitterness. Jealousy, competition and feelings of inadequacy seem to raise their ugly heads in every vocation—especially in the military, where leaders exercise authority over others.

Naaman heard them. He was aware of the scoffers who over the years had served under his command but lay in wait for an opportunity to "get back" at a leader. He turned his face and lowered his helmet as best he could. The chinstrap hid much of his face, so he made sure it stayed attached. He also grabbed at his collar and made a desperate attempt to hide the lower portion of his chin and face, mostly contaminated now with the dreaded skin-eating disease. He knew the disease was repulsive to others; he could not bear to look at himself either. He just had not imagined it would invade his entire body so quickly. The man who once stood so tall and spoke so boldly now cowered to some degree, yet his pride remained intact as he struggled to maintain a level of dignity.

What am I to do? Naaman was desperate. He thought of his wife. *I don't know how to face her—she hasn't seen me in days—now this horrid curse has affected my face. Wasn't it enough for it to consume my hands and fingers? How much longer before I am exiled from humanity?*

At home, Naaman's wife waited faithfully for her husband. Her new maid, an Israelite whom the Syrians had taken captive, waited on her. Though a foreigner, the maid seemed to take an interest in her mistress, and so Naaman's wife talked to her.

"I wonder what is taking Naaman so long to return home. The troops gathered in the city two days ago. Surely he is not in trouble! But maybe . . ."

"My mistress," the maid sat on her knees to untie her mistress's sandals, "do you think he is all right? Could he be ill?" The maid proceeded to bathe the dust from her mistress's feet.

"Yes." Naaman's wife stabilized herself in the chair as each foot was cleansed. She hesitated to offer more information—after all, leprosy was so humiliating and unclean. No one talked about a leper. And to expose a commander's condition would be considered betrayal.

"Well . . ." she paused once more and then decided to confide in her maid. "He has leprosy, and I am afraid he is losing all hope. When I last saw him the disease was spreading furiously. I shudder to think . . ." In her mind she was imagining the worst.

"Oh, I wish he would go see the prophet in Samaria!" The maid became excited as she anticipated a miracle. "I am sure the prophet could heal him!"

Finally Naaman arrived home. He slowly opened the door and peeked inside, and then, though it was customary to remove helmet and coat at the door, he walked in fully clothed. He glanced into the next room, where he saw his wife attended by her maid. The two were deep in conversation, and he dared not disturb her. And he needed more time before he would be ready to reveal his deterioration. Naaman waited a while, preparing his heart, and then approached the threshold.

"Naaman! Thank goodness you are . . ." She grew silent. Knowing she must guard her emotions, she took a deep breath and smiled. With every ounce of courage and determination, she drew near him. Grabbing his hand, which had only three fingers left, she lifted herself onto her toes and grazed his ravaged cheek with a slight kiss.

"Oh, my love." Tears swelled within her, and she fought them back, hoping he would not notice.

"Come! Sit." She made her way back to her seat. "Naaman, I was just talking to my maid. Please hear me out. She says that there is a prophet in Syria who has healing power. You must go to him!"

Naaman sank back into his chair, listening and then thinking. He dared not believe at first. He had heard of prophets who had been given power by God to heal others. But would the God of the Jews be willing to heal him, a Syrian? After a few moments he mustered up enough courage to look the maid in the eye, almost not caring anymore who was offended by his disfigured features.

"You must go to the king," his wife begged. "Tell him what my Israelite maid has said. She is a woman of great faith—it is your last hope for a miracle!"

"I will go." Naaman set his pride aside only for a brief moment and then asked, "Yet how can I allow the king to see me like this?"

To See the Prophet

Within a few days Naaman approached the king of Syria with his request. After seeing Naaman's condition, the king graciously heeded his plea for help and agreed to send a letter to the king of Israel asking for help for Naaman. Naaman left his presence with ten talents of silver, six thousand shekels of gold and ten changes of clothing.

He traveled to Israel, and then, once again mustering up his courage and raw nerve (and wearing his helmet and a high collar), Naaman went before the king of Israel. He read to him the letter from the king of Syria asking for the king of Israel to help Naaman receive his miracle.

The king grew angry and perplexed, and he rent his clothes to show his distress. "Who does your king think I am? He sent you to me to be healed of leprosy? Is he wanting some type of war and chooses this as the beginning?" The king paced the floor, ranting and raving over the expectation of the king of Syria.

When the prophet of God, Elisha, heard about this, he sent a letter to the king asking, "King of Israel, why have you rent your clothes? Send Naaman to me, and he will know that there is a prophet in Israel!"

In haste Naaman rode to Elisha's home, his entourage of horses and chariots following. Because of his position and because he was sent by two kings, he fully expected to meet Elisha personally, and upon arrival he sent his servant to knock at the prophet's quarters.

Elisha's servant answered the door. "Yes, whom do you seek?"

"The great commander Naaman has come so that Elisha may come out and heal him. Please tell your master that Naaman awaits. Go quickly to tell him that my master is waiting!"

After a brief time, Elisha's servant returned—without the prophet. The servant relayed a message from Elisha, who had discerned that Naaman's pride needed surrendering. The servant gave Elisha's instructions to Naaman: "Go and wash in the Jordan seven times, and your flesh shall be restored and you shall be clean."

"*Do what?*" Naaman grew angry. *He wants me to dip in unclean water to heal an unclean condition? I am already unclean—why would I want to dip in unclean water?*

This is preposterous. Naaman's pride escalated with every passing second. *No one with any dignity would dip in the Jordan—and do it seven times?* He was fuming.

"No way!" He spoke to his servant, "Why can't this man of God simply come out and wave his hand over me and heal me? I have heard stories where one of their leaders— was it Moses?—simply lifted a rod to do miracles. What is going on with this prophet? Either he can heal or he can't.

"Besides that, the Abana and Pharpar, the rivers in Damascus, are clean and pure and surrounded by fruitfulness. Why can't I go there, where others like myself—you know, those in higher positions—go to bathe?" In a rage, he turned away.

One of his servants drew near and said, "Sir, if the prophet had asked you to do some great thing that made you look good and appealed to your pride, wouldn't you do it? Why not just do as he asks, for you will surely still be healed and can walk off in great pride once more?"

Well, maybe this servant is right. It seems to be the only way. So Naaman went and dipped as instructed, seven times in the dirty Jordan River. But first he had to remove his cloak, helmet and collared shirt, revealing his horrible disfigurement to all who were watching. Although embarrassed, he was determined to go through with it.

Naaman dipped once, then looked at his hands and fingers. No change.

Twice, three times. Nothing.

Four times, then five, then six. Finally he dipped a seventh time.

Naaman rose up quickly after the last dip. He brought his hands up out of the water to examine them. All ten fingers appeared perfectly healthy before him, with no trace of leprosy. "My face!" He looked at his servant. "How is my face?"

"My master—you are healed!"

Naaman was clean, healed and restored. "There truly *is* a prophet in Israel!" the great man declared.

Naaman returned to Elisha and stood before him. "Now I know that there is no God in all the earth except the God of Israel. As a token of my appreciation, I want to pay you for your services. Please accept my gift." He held out an offering of money to the prophet.

But the wise prophet refused to take any money for his gift. Instead he charged Naaman to go home in peace.

"At least take these two mules. I can no longer go to the house of Rimmon, our Syrian god, to worship and offer sacrifices, because now I know that though his name means 'to be high' he is not higher than your God! Please accept these as my sacrifice since I am not making a sacrifice to Rimmon."

Again Elisha refused. He knew that accepting money or gifts would defile his motive as a true prophet and insult God. The power of God cannot be bought, and Elisha knew that. He once again sent Naaman away in peace, and Naaman departed.

Gehazi

Elisha's servant, Gehazi, had been observing the entire conversation. Gehazi envied Elisha's ability to hear from God and convinced himself that it would be the "religious" and "acceptable" thing to do to take up an offering after such a miraculous thing. Gehazi took off in a mad dash after Naaman, fully convinced he was doing what would be pleasing to God.

From a distance Naaman saw Gehazi approaching. He stopped his chariot and waited for Gehazi to catch up, then stepped down to meet him. "Is everything all right?"

Gehazi had to take a moment to catch his breath and then responded, "Yes, everything is fine." Gehazi then operated out of control and manipulation as he lied, "Sir, my master has sent me to say that two young sons of the prophets have arrived from Mt. Ephraim. Would you bless them with a talent of silver and two garment changes?"

"Be blessed to take two talents," Naaman replied. "It is the least I can do." He put the two talents of silver and two changes of clothing in two bags and had two of his servants carry them back for Gehazi.

Upon Gehazi's return to the top of the hill, he took the gifts from the two servants, put them in the house and sent the men away. Going back inside the house, he found Elisha waiting.

"Where have you been?" Elisha demanded.

"Nowhere."

"Did not my spirit go with you when Naaman turned from his chariot to meet you? Don't you know that the Lord tells His prophets the secret things?" Elisha was not prideful in saying these things. He only sought repentance from his servant.

"Did you feel you deserved payment? Have you made covenant with one of their Syrian gods—Mammon? Couldn't you wait for God's provision without attempting to steal it or lie about it to receive what you felt you deserved? Did you not trust me and discern that it was best not to take his gifts? Why then, if you trust me as your father in the Lord, did you run after them?" Elisha paused and grieved over this matter. "Was it a time to accept money, garments, olive orchards, vineyards, sheep, oxen or any other type of gift? Now because you have come into agreement with lies and deceit, therefore the leprosy of Naaman shall be upon you and the lives of your generations."

From that moment on Gehazi was a leper—as white as snow. He had been cursed for bowing to Mammon, manipulating and lying to Naaman and Elisha, and offending God.

The Battles of Naaman and Gehazi

Naaman struggled with the sin of pride. His high position made it difficult for him to stoop and bow down to the God of Elisha. But Naaman's high position of authority was not enough to sway Elisha. Elisha recognized what was in Naaman's heart and tested him. Naaman's test was whether or not he would submit to the Word of the Lord and believe that it was only by His hand that he would be healed. He had to face the sins of pride and unbelief and overcome them in order to walk in healing. Naaman did choose to believe, and he was able to cycle out of his wilderness and into his promise.

Furthermore, Naaman had to be exposed in public. In order to get to his healing, he had to reveal his illness first to his wife and her maid, then to his king, then to the king of Israel, then to Elisha and his servant, and finally to all who watched him bathe in the Jordan. Sometimes God chooses ways to heal us that seem a bit challenging, to say the least. He exposes us in public. He asks us to walk down the aisle during a church altar call, for example. Or He pushes us to attend a corporate deliverance service. We may want to choose an alternate plan, but God is the One in charge, and we must do it His way. After, all our ways are not His ways, and His ways are always higher.

Gehazi, on the other hand, was not able to step into His promise. He found himself in a major battle with Mammon. Avarice and greed overtook him, and he listened to the voice of the evil one rather than God. Instead of obeying the authority over him, Gehazi sneakily circumvented that authority, lied to Naaman and then lied to Elisha, all the while motivated by Mammon. Subsequently both he and his generations were cursed by God.

Does this story hit too close to home? Are your unclean areas being challenged? Do you wish you could lay down this book and walk away? Dear ones, if it is hitting that close, then God wants to do a work inside your "house." He wants to heal your heart.

Ananias and Sapphira

Another account in the Bible directly addresses the seductions of Mammon and its ability to deceive God's prophets, leaders and people. This story, however, has a completely different setting. And again, it hits close to home.

It was the time of the early Church. Miraculous events had been occurring, the Holy Spirit was moving in a powerful way and all the believers were of one heart and mind. No one felt as if what he owned belonged to him individually, for everyone was sharing (see Acts 4:32). The apostles were preaching powerful sermons concerning the resurrection, people were fellowshipping with one another like true family and there was absolutely no poverty among them. Everyone who owned land or houses was selling them and laying the money at the feet of the apostles to give to others in need. It was an amazing move of God.

Ananias and his wife, Sapphira, were members of the early Church (see Acts 5). They, too, sold some property, but rather than giving the entire profit to the apostles as everyone else had, they brought only a portion and hoarded the rest for themselves. These two were seduced by Mammon. But if they had been honest about what they were doing, it would not have been so bad. Instead, when Ananias gave the portion to the apostles he claimed that he was giving the full price they had received for the sale of their possession. In other words, he lied outright, falling even deeper into Mammon's trap.

When Ananias lied, Peter's discernment kicked in, and Peter told him:

> Satan has filled your heart. When you claimed this was the full price, you were lying to the Holy Spirit. The property was yours to sell or not, as you wished. And after selling it, it was yours to decide how much to give. How could you do a thing like this? You weren't lying to us, but to God.
>
> Acts 5:3–4, TLB

In other words, Ananias did not have to sell his property as the others did. Whether he sold it or not was not the issue. The issue was that he lied to make it appear that he was doing what everyone else was. Not only was Mammon involved here, but Ananias's pride was, too. He and Sapphira desired to appear as spiritual as the others. They knew there was anointing upon the "oneness" in the Spirit. They desired to be treated as part of the family of believers but did not want to pay the same price. Dear ones, this type of lie causes a death structure to be erected. In fact, Ananias dropped to the floor dead.

Talk about a holy fear that came upon the people! The men covered him with a sheet and took him out immediately to bury him.

About three hours later, Sapphira showed up, not knowing what had occurred. Peter gave her a really pointed pop quiz and asked her if she and Ananias had sold their land for the price Ananias had quoted. She, too, lied and answered yes. Peter responded, "How is it that ye have agreed together to tempt the Spirit of the Lord? Behold, the feet of them which have buried thy husband are at the door, and shall carry thee out" (Acts 5:9, KJV). And Sapphira immediately fell down dead and was buried beside her husband.

There is no biblical record of that occurring again. I can certainly understand why, can't you?

When Ananias and Sapphira received their financial breakthrough, their hearts were seduced by Mammon and their motives were weighed in the balance. Their love of money overcame their love for God. When Mammon is involved, our true motives toward building God's Kingdom become challenged.

As leaders in the Body of Christ, Mickey and I have seen this happen often in the Church. People who truly love God will promise to bless God's Kingdom "when our ship comes in." Praying for a financial breakthrough, they make all kinds of promises to God and church leaders. But when the ship does dock, Mammon steps in and God often does not receive the money that was promised to Him. Babylon, too, begins to operate and bring confusion as to what they should do, to whom they should give and even whether or not they should give at all. Dear ones, Mammon and

Babylon are used powerfully by Satan to distract us from Kingdom giving and Kingdom living.

How would you respond if you received a large amount of money? Would you respond properly with tithes and offerings? Or would you fall prey to the spirit of Mammon, who seeks to distract you from your Kingdom purpose?

Oh, I pray that we all would respond in love and faith!

Tearing Down the Altars of the Enemy

Though you may not have fully understood the seductions of Mammon before, I pray your eyes are being opened to the wiles of our enemy. I pray that these biblical accounts are hitting close to home and that God is revealing any uncleanness in your heart.

If I have fully gotten your attention now, then I encourage you to pray the following prayer to tear down the altars of the enemy and take steps to repair the altar of God in your life:

Lord, I repent for and renounce the sins of pride, doubt and unbelief concerning Your ability to provide and care for me. I recognize that my heart is unclean. I repent for the sin of covetousness and the sin of independence. I renounce the sin of a haughty look and attitude concerning what "I think is best" for my life.

I repent for believing that "I have a better way" than Your divine will and directives for my life. Forgive me for any attempt to keep my sin hidden, thus giving place to occult roots. I repent for rejecting my inheritance as God's child. I believe that as I repent the seed of doubt and unbelief that the enemy planted is being destroyed and the altars of the enemy are being torn down.

I choose to surrender my life to You. I choose to believe You and Your Word. You are exalted above all—especially above the spirit of Mammon. You are empowering me to crush the seeds of Satan and replace them with the implanted Word of God.

I now declare that I will arise in the name of Jesus and take my rightful position in the authority of Christ. I declare that no weapon formed against me will prosper and that Your Word says You will cause all things to work together for my good. I choose to allow Your purifying fires to cleanse my heart, to be circumcised and buried with Christ. I fully submit to Your divine plan for my life.

In the mighty name of Jesus Christ, Amen.

I know that your heart has often been challenged as you have received the revelation contained in this book, just as mine has. Every page of this book has been soaked in tears and intercession. I have walked through every trial and tribulation and fasted for each of you. I desire only God's best for each of you. I want you to be free—totally free. If you truly desire that, too, then join me for our final chapter!

10

Repairing the Altar of God

The word of the LORD came to Elijah:
"Go and present yourself to Ahab, and I
will send rain on the land."

1 Kings 18:1

Elijah, the Tishbite from Tishbe in Gilead, went forth
to meet King Ahab. He neither hurried nor dragged
his feet but steadily paced himself with fierce determination
to remain obedient to his directive from the Lord.

Just three years earlier Elijah had confronted Ahab with
the Word of the Lord: "As the LORD, the God of Israel,
lives, whom I serve, there will be neither dew nor rain in

the next few years except at my word" (1 Kings 17:1). All rain had stopped, and drought overshadowed the lands of Israel and Samaria; death and famine were rampant. Ahab had issued a death warrant for Elijah, the prophet who had declared devastation on Israel. To protect Elijah's life, God had directed him to leave and hide.

As Elijah went again to meet Ahab in obedience to the Lord, his faith dwindled a bit and he prayed, *Lord God, I will remain steady and continue to serve You with a fervent passion, but I am recalling the last time I confronted Ahab. He wants to kill me, Lord! Do I actually have to see him to make this declaration? I could merely spread out my arm in the direction of Israel—you know, like Moses did with his rod?*

Elijah felt fear rising and then immediately captured his thoughts. He began to recall the last few years of his life. *It is a miracle I am still alive, Lord. First You have me declare a drought, then to protect me from the effects of my own declaration You send me away to hide in the Cherith Ravine, east of the Jordan.*

Elijah continued toward Israel, remembering how God had ordered ravens to feed him. *Ravens! Imagine that! You fed me by ravens.* His faith began to strengthen once more. *And You daily gave me water at the brook. Even when that brook dried up You still had provision prepared ahead for me.* He recalled how the Lord had sent him to the widow in Zarepath. *She was gathering sticks when I met her. She was preparing what she thought was her last meal, and then she thought she and her son were going to die. Lord, I cannot believe You told me to be so bold as to tell her to give me her last meal! And she did. You are so good, Lord. You saved the three of us with Your provision of grain and oil that did not run out. I know*

You anointed me then, Lord. Please anoint me again when I meet Ahab.

He remembered, too, how God had enabled him to raise the widow's son from death in her upper room. *Lord, You used me to raise the dead. I can do anything through Your power! I know that You will not fail me and what You ask me to do and speak, I will surely do.*

Elijah entered Samaria. The drought was so severe that it was difficult for him not to focus on the devastation. But he remained focused on the task at hand.

On the road he met Obadiah, who was in charge of Ahab's palace. Obadiah had remained a faithful servant of the Lord, hiding multitudes of the Lord's prophets as Jezebel, Ahab's queen, sought to kill every one. By now Elijah had pushed past his fears. He had faith in God's ability to protect him and use him for His glory, and he was ready to meet Ahab. He told Obadiah, "Go and tell Ahab that Elijah is here."

"I cannot do that!" Obadiah exclaimed. "He will kill me! If I tell him you are here and God takes you off somewhere else, then King Ahab will be so angry that he will destroy me."

"Calm down, Obadiah," Elijah quieted him. "As surely as the Lord Almighty lives, I will present myself to Ahab today. I give you my word: I will remain here." In obedience Obadiah left and went to tell Ahab what Elijah had said.

When Ahab confronted Elijah, he pointed his finger at him and said, "Is that you, you troubler of Israel?" It was hard for Ahab to refrain from grabbing Elijah by the throat, for he was convinced that the cause of the drought lay in Elijah's power. He did not understand that God was angry with Ahab and that it was God who caused the suffering of Israel, not Elijah. The prophet was merely the messenger.

Still, Ahab hated and blamed Elijah for the tragic condition of Israel. Oh, if only Ahab had understood the power of repentance. Yet his marriage to the evil Jezebel caused him to be seduced into idolatry, along with the entire nation of Israel. It was for this reason that God had punished Ahab and the nation.

"I have not made trouble for Israel," Elijah defended himself and remained firm. "Ahab, it was you and your father's family. You have abandoned the Lord's commands and followed the Baals. You have worshiped false gods and bowed your knee to them. Now summon the people from all over Israel to meet me on Mount Carmel."

Elijah turned to leave. Then he suddenly turned back and pointed at Ahab. "Oh, Ahab, and also bring the four hundred and fifty prophets of Baal and four hundred and fifty prophets of Asherah who eat at your queen's table." The anointing was so heavy upon Elijah that the words of the Lord were out of his mouth before he even realized what he had said.

Lord, he prayed, *I stand prepared for what You would have me do. I am sure that I am to confront the false gods of Israel, tear down their idols and rebuild Your altar in the land. Israel has turned from You and built idols in Your temples, and now I will tear them down and rebuild Your divine altar. You are Lord, and I know that You will remove Your people from the stench of sin, destroy the lies attached to false worship and restore truth in the land.*

Ahab sent word through all of Israel and assembled the false prophets on Mount Carmel. He could not believe he was accommodating the one who had caused all this trouble! But Ahab assumed that Elijah had something to say to the false prophets, and he had no idea of what really lay ahead on Mount Carmel. Holding back his anger, Ahab followed through with Elijah's directives.

Then Ahab realized that Mount Carmel was surrounded by jungles of dwarf-oaks and olives that could furnish abundant wood for an altar to Elijah's God. *He is going to build the Lord an altar!* Ahab gasped for air and shuddered as he thought, *What will Jezebel say about this?*

A short time later the people had gathered. Seeing the crowd from a distance, Elijah knew it was his time to confront God's enemy. "Lord, empower me to do Your divine will." Boldly he walked in front of the crowd and proclaimed confidently, "How long will you waver between two opinions? If the LORD is God, follow him; but if Baal is God, follow him" (1 Kings 18:21).

How Long Will We Waver?

Dear ones, the crux of this entire book is embodied in this one statement by Elijah. How long will we waver between two opinions? If the Lord is God, then we must follow Him. But if Satan is our god, then we must follow him. We cannot serve two masters.

As we consider the seductions of Mammon and Babylon, we must make a choice. If we remain in confusion and doubt God's desire to bless, prosper and love us, then we are choosing to allow Babylon to seduce us and cause us to bow down. Remember, *Babylon* means "confusion." When we doubt God, we are confused about His faithfulness. If, on the other hand, we know that God is truly God, then we are bound to serve Him.

Choose to believe Him! If you do choose to believe His Word, then stand up right now and say, "Lord, I believe

You and not the voice of the enemy!" Say it—right now, out loud. When Elijah confronted the people, they said nothing (see 1 Kings 18:21). They just stood by the altars of their false gods. By making a firm, faith-filled declaration, you will tear down the false altars that have been built by your being in agreement with the enemy.

Beloved, I see myself placing your hand in the hand of our Savior. He will walk with you the rest of the way.

Now let me ask you again: How long will you waver between two opinions?

Tearing Down False Altars and Repairing the Altar of the Lord

Elijah had the people build an altar to their false god. He instructed them to choose a bull, prepare it for sacrifice and then call on the name of their false god. They were not, however, to light the fire for the sacrifice to be consumed.

The false prophets of Baal called on his name from morning until noon. "Oh, Baal, answer us!" They shouted and danced, hoping to be answered with fire to prove that Baal was God. There was no response.

Midday passed, and still no response from Baal. The false prophets began to prophesy frantically and cut themselves until blood flowed. Finally at evening they began to give up. Dear ones, when we give up our old belief systems, which have been built on falsehoods, and we turn to recognize that God truly is Lord and is faithful, then false altars come a-tumblin' down!

Elijah rose up and told the people that it was time to "repair the altar of the Lord." Now you must understand that the altar of the Lord was in ruins. It had been a long time since Israel had truly worshiped God with their whole hearts and minds. They had sought other gods, building idols that promised provision and fruitfulness, rather than serving the One True God.

Now, dear ones, I am going to ask you to do some more self-examination here. Ask yourself: Do I need to repair my prayer altar? As we take a close look at the repairing of the altar of the Lord, see if you can relate to what needs rebuilding or repairing in your life.

The repair of the altar went like this (see 1 Kings 18:30–39):

1. Elijah took twelve stones, one for each of the tribes of Israel, and built the foundation for the altar.

   Let me ask you to examine your foundation. Does your belief system totally align with the Word? Is there any area of doubt and unbelief, any confusion, any addiction or lie that you keep believing? If the foundation is not firm, then you will continue to be double-minded and waver. Remember, as a man thinks in his heart, he becomes. Allow God to continue to show you the way to divine fulfillment.

2. Elijah dug a trench around the altar large enough to hold two measures of seed. This is important because Elijah dug a trench for the water that he knew was going to fill it.

   Similarly, we must be prepared for the Living Water to remain at our altar of sacrifice and worship. Without the Living Water, there is no life. If we do not keep "digging ditches," God is not going to fill them. He wants us daily to dig a ditch in our lives through prayer so that He can come and fill us. Then He desires to plant the seed in our spirits. What is the seed? It is the Lord; He is the seed that impregnates us with our future. God desires to overshadow us during our prayer time and worship time—actually any time!—and impregnate us with His Word.

3. Elijah then arranged the wood, cut the sacrificial bull into pieces and laid the pieces on the wood.

God is putting our lives into place. It is true that we die daily. We must lay down our lives as a living sacrifice—yet when we do, He comes and fills us to overflowing with His life. How dare we continue to complain about how "hard" life is! How dare we not trust Him for our fulfillment, provision, healing and abundance as He promised. We must not waver another moment. Lay it down—lay down your burden right now. Let the old altars of unbelief crumble down, and trust wholly in the Lord.

4. Elijah then told them to fill four large jars with water and pour it on the offering and the wood. Three times Elijah ordered the water to drench the sacrifice, and the water ran down the sacrifice and filled the trench. Three is the number for completion. This was so the sacrifice would be totally saturated. This act was meant to testify to God's power to send fire from heaven and totally consume the sacrifice.

As you continue to prepare your new altar unto God and as you lay down your life, your heart must be ready for His holy fire to totally consume you and burn away all mistrust, doubt, unbelief, etc. You must be completely consumed with Him. Set your face like flint right now and declare that you will not crawl down from the altar until God has burnt you like a "crispy critter!" Believe me, doing so will keep you from cycling back into another wilderness.

5. Elijah asked God to answer him so that the people would know that He was God and that He was "turning their hearts back to Him."

Dear ones, the need to rebuild the altar is because He wants to turn our hearts. Oh, how He loves us!

Of course, the fire of the Lord fell and burned up the sacrifice, the wood, the stones, the soil and even the water in the trench. Think about it: God so wanted to turn their hearts that His holy passion became a fire that totally consumed the altar—even the stones and the dirt. Then the fire drained the trenches—now that is hot fire. And God's miraculous demonstration proved His determination to show Israel His power.

Surrender

Dear ones, God is this passionate concerning you, too. He wants to consume your life. Will you let Him?

You are now at the turning point of making the right choices. Will you choose life or death? God or Mammon? Will you surrender?

My season with you in this book is over. And I surrender now to the precious Holy Spirit:

Holy Spirit, I consider it such a privilege to once more co-labor with You. I thank You for Your direction during this season. You have always been faithful to speak whenever

I quieted my spirit long enough. Now, Holy Spirit, these readers are in Your care for You to continue to teach them and guide them in all trust. Lord Jesus, I know that You will continue to direct each reader to the Father. I pray for each reader and that You empower them with complete abandonment to seek You and Your perfect will for their lives. In Jesus' name, Amen.

Readers, I love you all! May God's glory shine upon you, and may you continue to follow after Him!

In His service always,
Sandie

Notes

Chapter 1 God and Mammon

1. Noah Webster, *American Dictionary of the English Language* (Chesapeake, Va.: Foundation for American Christian Education, Seventeenth Printing, 2005), "mammon."

2. Albert Barnes, *Barnes' Notes* (Biblesoft, Inc., Electronic Database, 1997, 2003), "Mammon."

3. *The Bible Illustrator* (Ages Software, Inc., and Biblesoft, Inc., 2002, 2003), "Mammon."

4. *Biblesoft's New Exhaustive Strong's Numbers and Concordance with Expanded Greek-Hebrew Dictionary* (Biblesoft, Inc., and International Bible Translators, Inc., 1994, 2003), 1398, 1401.

5. Ibid.

6. Carol and Jerry Robeson, *Strongman's His Name . . . What's His Game?* (Woodburn, Ore.: Shiloh Publishing House, 1996), 102–3.

7. *Biblesoft's New Exhaustive Strong's,* 3308, 3309.

8. Ibid.

9. Ibid, 3689.

Chapter 2 Babylon and Wealth

1. Sandie Freed, *Strategies from Heaven's Throne: Claiming the Life God Wants for You* (Grand Rapids: Chosen Books, 2007), 107.

2. Matthew Henry, *Matthew Henry's Commentary of the Whole Bible* (Peabody, Mass.: Henderson Publishers, 1992, "The First Book of Moses, Genesis"), "Genesis 10:8–10."

3. Jane Hamon, *The Cyrus Decree* (Santa Rosa Beach, Fla.: Christian International, 2004), 11.

4. Henry, Genesis 10:8–10.

5. *Fausset's Bible Dictionary* (Electronic Database, Biblesoft, 1998, 2003), "Babylon."

6. Ibid.

7. *Wikipedia Free Online Dictionary* (Wikimedia Foundation), Wikipedia.org/wiki/occult.

8. Chuck Pierce and Rebecca Wagner Systema, *The Future War of the Church* (Ventura, Calif.: Regal Books, 2007), 104–5.

9. Dr. Judson Cornwall and Dr. Stelman Smith, *The Exhaustive Dictionary of Bible Names* (North Brunswick, N.J.: Bridge-Logos, 1998), p. 100 and *Biblesoft's New Exhaustive Strong's*, 5674.

10. Freed, *Strategies,* 37–38.

11. Ibid.

12. *International Standard Bible Encyclopedia* (Electronic Database, Biblesoft, Inc., 1996, 2003), "Babylon."

13. Ibid.

14. Hamon, *Cyrus Decree*, 9.

Chapter 3 Iniquity, Tyre and Seats of Authority

1. *Biblesoft's New Exhaustive Strong's,* 5771, 5753.

2. Ibid.

3. Pierce and Systema, *Future War of the Church*, 111.

4. Merrill F. Unger, *Unger's Bible Dictionary* (Chicago: Moody Press, 1957), 844.

5. Boyd Rice, www.thevesselofgod.com/hiram.html.

6. Cindy Jacobs, *Exposing the Gates of the Enemy* (Grand Rapids: Chosen Books, 1994), 227.

7. Neil T. Anderson and Rich Miller, *Walking in Freedom* (Ventura, Calif.: Regal Publishers, 1999).

Chapter 4 Understanding the Deceitfulness of Riches

1. *Biblesoft's New Exhaustive Strong's*, 4624, 4625.

2. Ibid, 4846.

3. Ibid, 539.

4. Ibid, 1411, 2570.

5. Ibid, 7105.

Chapter 5 Our Treasure Is Where Our Hearts Are

1. *Biblesoft's New Exhaustive Strong's*, 2344.

2. Ibid.

3. Ibid.

4. Ibid, 5911.

5. Webster, "trouble."

6. *Biblesoft's New Exhaustive Strong's*, 3309.

7. Ibid, 3667.

8. Johnny Enlowe, *The Seven Mountain Prophecy: Unveiling the Coming Elijah Revolution* (Lake Mary, Fla.: Creation House, 2008), 102.

9. Barnes, *Barnes' Notes,* Matthew 6:19.

Chapter 6 Is There an Ammonite in Your Treasury?

1. Sandie Freed, *Breaking the Threefold Demonic Cord: How to Discern and Defeat the Lies of Jezebel, Athaliah and Delilah* (Grand Rapids: Chosen Books, 2008).

2. Cornwall and Smith, *Exhaustive Dictionary,* 209.

3. Ibid, 240.

4. Ibid, 78.

5. Wikipedia, "Ammon."

Chapter 7 Anointed to Defeat Mammon, Babylon and Divination

1. Fausset's, "Damascus."

2. Ibid.

3. Sandie Freed, *Conquering the Antichrist Spirit: Discerning and Defeating the Seducer That Binds Believers Today* (Grand Rapids: Chosen Books, 2009).

4. Strong's, 1278, 1223, 4192.

5. Strong's, 4436.

6. Webster's, "discernment."

7. Barnes, *Barnes' Notes,* Micah 3:11 and Proverbs 16:10.

Chapter 8 It Is Written!

1. James W. Goll and Lou Engle, *Elijah Revolution: The Call to Passion and Sacrifice for Radical Change* (Shippensburg, Penn.: Treasure House/Destiny Image Publishers, 2002), 135.

2. Webster's, "delusion."

3. Wikipedia, "seven deadly sins."

Sandie Freed and her husband, Mickey, are the founders and directors of Zion Ministries in Hurst, Texas. Together they pastored a local church in Texas for more than fourteen years, and today they apostolically oversee the Zion Kingdom Training Center, which trains and activates the Body of Christ in the fivefold ministries and spiritual giftings.

In addition, Mickey and Sandie have launched Win Ministries in Hurst, Texas, a nonprofit organization to empower women in need. Davis House has been established through Zion Ministries not only to house unwed mothers and women seeking counseling and deliverance, but also to provide spiritual mentoring and impartation.

Sandie is an ordained prophetess with Christian International Ministries and travels extensively teaching prophetic truths to the Body of Christ. She has written five other books: *Conquering the Antichrist Spirit: Discerning and Defeating the Seducer That Binds Believers Today*; *Breaking the Threefold Demonic Cord: How to Discern and Defeat the Lies of Jezebel, Athaliah and Delilah*; *Destiny Thieves: Defeat Seducing Spirits and Achieve Your Purpose in God*; *Strategies from Heaven's Throne: Claiming the Life God Wants for You* and *Dream On: Unlocking Your Dreams and Visions*.

Sandie has a master's degree in biblical theology and is presently pursuing a doctorate. She is often a featured guest on television and radio, where she has shared her testimony of God's healing and delivering power. As a gifted minister in prophecy, interpreting dreams and visions with keen spiritual discernment, Sandie is a sought-after speaker and seminar instructor for her leadership skills, her ability to interpret dreams and visions, and her discernment of strongholds over individuals, churches and regions. She is known for powerful, down-to-earth messages that release life transformation and encouragement to church leaders and the Body of Christ.

To contact Sandie regarding speaking engagements, you may reach her at:

Zion Ministries
P.O. Box 5487
Hurst, TX 76054
(817) 589-8811 or (817) 284-5966
email: zionministries1@sbcglobal.net
website: www.zioministries.us

For more information on Win Ministries or Zion Ministries seminars such as "The School of Prophets," "Advanced Prophetic Training" and "Prophetic Intercession Training," or to see recent teaching, books, tapes or Sandie's itinerary, log onto the Zion Ministries website.

One of Satan's secret weapons is gaining alarming momentum among believers: the threefold cord of Jezebel, Athaliah and Delilah—demonic spirits that bind us to our pasts. Through a divine prayer strategy, Sandie Freed shows you how to discern and defeat these spirits—severing their demonic cord—to claim your righteous destiny.

Breaking the Threefold Demonic Cord

Since the birth of Christianity, a demonic system has infiltrated society—and even Christian beliefs— denying the supremacy of Christ and keeping believers confused, anxious and lacking in authority. But no more. This is your manual to freedom. With piercing insight, Sandie Freed exposes this stronghold and lays out a practical battle plan that will empower you to put every demonic force under your feet.

Conquering the Antichrist Spirit

Take Hold
of Your Destiny

God is offering you a destiny greater than any you have ever dreamed, but Satan is working relentlessly to distract, seduce and shame you into defeat. With a call for discernment and holiness, Sandie Freed shows you how to thwart the plans of the destiny-thieves spirits, ultimately defeating them and enjoying the destiny that is rightfully yours.

Destiny Thieves

When God works a miracle, it is a thrilling experience—and He expects us to join Him in it! Sharing from her own experience, Sandie Freed offers practical advice on being free from religious expectations that limit God's plans, showing how you can discern God's voice, release the past and move forward to possess the life He has planned for you.

Strategies from Heaven s Throne